STAR TREK
THE NEXT GENERATION®

CUSTOMIZABLE™
CARD GAME

DECIPHER INC.

BradyGAMES

Copyright 1995
Paramount Pictures

Brady Publishing

An Imprint of
Macmillan Computer Publishing
201 West 103rd Street
Indianapolis, Indiana 46290

ISBN: 1-56686-248-5
Library of Congress Catalog No.: 94-073762
98 97 96 95   4 3 2 1

Manufactured in the United States of America.

Credits

Publisher
Rick Ranucci

Managing Editor
Debra Kempker

Acquisitions Manager
Sarah Browning

Project Editor
David Bartley

Technical Editor
Tom Braunlich

Associate Editor
Debra McBride

Designer
Kevin Spear

Cover Designer
Jean Bisesi

Imprint Manager
Kelly Dobbs

Marketing Coordinator
Monica Cronin

Production Team
Gary Adair, Dan Caparo, Kim Cofer,
Jennifer Eberhardt, Dave Eason, Rob
Falco, Erika Millen, Beth Rago, Karen
Walsh, Robert Wolf

About the Authors

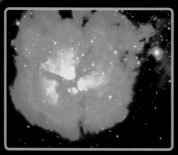

Tom Braunlich is president of Technical Game Services, Inc. and, in conjunction with partner Rollie Tesh, was one of the designers of the Star Trek: The Next Generation Customizable Card Game. Tom has written seven books on game design and strategy. A graduate of Oklahoma State University with a degree in Journalism, he lives now in Virginia and devotes his full attention to making the Star Trek universe come alive through cards.

Bill Muldowney is a former high school English teacher, academic dean, and corporate training manager. He is currently a training consultant with Dale Carnegie in central New York. Bill is an avid *Star Trek: The Next Generation* fan and has been playing ST:TNG Customizable Card Game since it was first introduced. He has a 12-year-old son named Michael and lives in Syracuse, New York.

I would like to thank my son, Michael, who is the inspiration for almost everything I do. He's helped me to never forget the child in me.

—Bill Muldowney

Contents

Foreword

When Gene Roddenberry created *Star Trek*® more than twenty-five years ago, he introduced us to a galaxy of characters that dramatically influenced and enriched our lives. *Star Trek*® embodies the ultimate quest of the human race... to expand our knowledge, explore new worlds and experience life's many adventures.

The *Star Trek: The Next Generation*® Customizable™ Card Game invites you to begin an adventure—and millions of players have done just that. Only four months after the game's introduction, more than a quarter of a billion cards had been sold. (That's as close to warp speed as it gets on planet Earth!) To give you a mental picture of how staggering this is, consider this virtual mind-trip... look out your window and imagine placing those cards end-to-end along the ground as you walk. When your virtual feet are exhausted, you have traveled around the entire lower forty-eight United States, and you still carry over one hundred and thirty tons of cards on your shoulders (so your virtual back is exhausted, too!).

Just as no Starfleet officer would embark upon a mission without training, no player should begin this game without tactical guidance. This book serves as an excellent introduction to a variety of basic strategies. Since the game is relatively new, the options are constantly evolving. There is much to explore.

The authors, designers, and players themselves are discovering new alternatives every day. Once your trek with this book is completed, I encourage you to continue your exploration in this universe... *to boldly go where no one has gone before*™.

Scientists have been telling us for years that the universe is expanding. This is certainly true for the *Star Trek: The Next Generation*® *Customizable*™ Card Game universe. As we introduce expansion sets—like *Alternative Universe*, *Q-Continuum*, and *Holodeck Adventures*—players will gain strategic options, tactical abilities, and creative powers not yet imagined. You will truly be able to *expand your power in the Universe*™.

Being a guardian of Gene Roddenberry's vision is a great responsibility. I am very lucky to be working with the most talented people in this industry—Dan Burns, Ross Campbell, Cindy Thornburg, Tom Braunlich, Rollie Tesh, Darwin Bromley, the Product Development team at Paramount, and many more people too numerous to mention. We are all committed to making your game-playing experience an exciting one.

Welcome to a universe with endless possibilities.

Warren Holland
President
Decipher Inc.

ENTERING THE STAR TREK UNIVERSE

The History of Star Trek: The Next Generation Customizable Card Game

Design Notes by Tom Braunlich

"Oh, by the way . . .," said my business partner, Rollie Tesh, as he leaned into my office one November afternoon in 1993, "While I was on the phone with Darwin Bromley, he said there's a new game out we should know about. It's becoming a huge hit."

"Sure," I said. As licensing agents for the major game companies, people make that kind of claim to us all the time. However, it usually doesn't come from an experienced designer like Darwin Bromley, president of Mayfair Games, who knows better than to make wild assertions.

"It's called *Magic*. It came out a few months ago by some small company in Seattle. It's supposed to be flying off the shelves."

"If it's so great, how come we've never heard of it?"

"It's being sold only in the hobby/adventure game market. It's a huge card game with hundreds of cards, but it's packaged like trading cards."

Within a month it was clear that with the trend started by *Magic: The Gathering*, the game industry was witnessing the development of the first new game category in over 10 years. It was to be a category that would come to dominate our lives in 1994 and beyond, starting us on our own 5-year mission into the *Star Trek* universe. Here is a brief history of how the *Star Trek: The Next Generation Customizable Card Game* came about....

A New Game Genre

The traditional game industry has been in the doldrums since the 1970s, under the growing domination of video and computer games. Except for the big spike of Trivial Pursuit, the game companies have for the most part been resorting to gimmicks, licensed characters, and "flashy" play in an attempt to attract players away from video. The last "new genre" to enter the gameplay world was *Dungeons and Dragons* in the early 70s.

Magic: The Gathering was a ground-breaking card game. It did what *Dungeons and Dragons* did for role playing games, and what *Scrabble* did for word games. Soon, other game designers, inspired by the new possibilities inherent in a new approach to gaming, were clamoring to enter this new market with designs of their own.

The new genre, which has come to be called "collectible card games" (or CCGs for short), combined known game elements in a particularly effective way. It is essentially a card game combined with "trading cards."

Each of the hundreds of cards is visually appealing and collectible, and each also has a special gameplay function. Players can only buy some of the cards at a time, since they are packaged semi-randomly like trading cards. To play, they "customize" a deck from all the cards in their collection. Players naturally want to increase the strength of their deck, and so they seek out other players to trade for cards they want, adding another dimension to the fun.

Beaming up to Star Trek

The best chance for a new CCG, as we saw it, was for a more mass market theme and approach. After all, we do most of our design business with the large mass market companies, so it was natural for us to try to visualize the problem from their point of view. They would want a theme with wide appeal.

After floundering around for a few weeks, the solution suddenly materialized—*Star Trek*! *Star Trek* has a rich universe of characters and mystery, with the "depth" needed to support hundreds of card possibilities. Since so many people are intimately familiar with the show, the game will have fewer complexity problems—if the game plays like the show, people already understand it.

Rollie took on the challenge of trying to sell this concept to one of the major game companies. It was December, and the large game companies debut their new products each February at the International Toy Fair in New York. The time line was impossibly short. These companies had decided on their 1994 products six months ago, and could not commit so quickly to something which could easily be a fad. Remember, despite its enormous sales, CCGs were still unheard of in the mass market game industry channels.

But we were able to convince one major game company to give it a try—Decipher, Inc. They were really the perfect company for this mission, as Rollie was finally able to convince them! They already had a close relationship with Paramount Pictures, owners of *Star Trek*, having done other games like their *Star Trek: VCR Board Game* series.

Decipher was a large enough company to have mass market distribution, yet small and flexible enough to work within the specialty markets. They had the entrepreneurial spirit to move quickly, and the computer skill to do a quality job. Plus, they had been close friends of ours for many years, having published several of our games previously. We knew we could work well together under tight deadlines.

By late December they were convinced of the potential of this new genre, and that *Star Trek* was the perfect topic for them. It was time to "Make it so!"

What happened after that is just a warp-speed blur. Cindy Thornburg, Vice President at Decipher, broke all speed records by getting a license from Paramount on ultra-short notice. Decipher's art department kicked-in its plasma injectors, full blast. Dan Burns heads the talented staff powered by a fleet of Macintosh hotrods—one of the best computer art departments in the business. They created mockups and catalog sheets in time for the game's debut in February.

And a name was born—the *Star Trek: The Next Generation Customizable Card Game* (which I abbreviate as ST:TNG CCG).

Creating a CCG "Ecosystem"

Building a CCG for *Star Trek: The Next Generation* proved to be a tough challenge—not unlike trying to design a living ecosystem from scratch. Designing any CCG is a lot more difficult than it seems, and it seems pretty difficult! The advantage of CCGs is that each card in the game says what it does. In a normal card game, you need rules to say what you can do with each card, which players must memorize. In a CCG, the rules only talk about the general structure of the game and the methods of play. The specific rules for each card are printed right on that card, telling you what you can do with it through symbols, numbers, and very brief explanations. Thus, it is fairly easy to understand how a CCG plays, because you only have to understand the basic structure of the game, not the details of each card. Like all good games, however, the tactical and strategical ramifications of these cards are deep—infinite card combinations provide unending variety in game play.

Thus, the way the game works is pretty straightforward. The difficulty in design comes from the plethora of ways the individual cards interact. This is a phenomenon you might call "matrix ramifications." Each card in the CCG creates a matrix of inter-related card effects. As in ecosystems and other complex systems, if you make a change in one card, it affects the whole system, the entire matrix.

If you think of each card as a new rule for the game, then each time you add a card, the ramifications of this rule change pro-pogate across the entire matrix of cards—like a new species invading an ecosystem.

When you consider adding (or removing) a card, you have to re-evaluate all the other cards that currently exist to see how the change will affect them. It is surprisingly easy for an apparently harmless new card to have major ramifications. This is especially subtle when the effects are indirect. For example, the introduction of card #300 to a game will alter the effects of card #112, which when played in combination with card #61 allows you to suddenly be able to destroy enemy ship cards with ease.

In fact, it is virtually impossible to predict all the ramifications for the interactions of hundreds of such cards. If you try to control the ramifications too much, the game will lose its vitality.

As it turns out, the ecosystem metaphor is again the key. One must try to build in natural checks and balances to the game, a basic flexibility that creates a balance such that no one card can turn out to be so unbalanced that it ruins the game. This balance is somewhat similar to the balance between predator and prey, animals and plants in an ecosystem. The basic game structure, in other words, has built-in possibilities to handle cards that are found to have undesirable ramifications.

Still, not everything can be foreseen, and inevitably some cards will need a backup method of balance. If a card is proven to be too strong due to unforeseen uses, future "expansion sets" can include "remedy" cards that re-balance the situation.

Encounter at Farpoint

The playability goals for the design created further challenges.

First, as *Star Trek* fans ourselves, we were determined to capture the flavor of Gene Roddenberry's rich fictional universe. We wanted to reproduce the appeal of *Star Trek* in the game, so that players could experience it directly, as if they were watching a new episode. This required achieving a high degree of realism and accuracy, which, in turn, demanded a completely different type of gameplay than that used in *Magic* (which is abstract and battle-oriented) or other CCGs known at the time. In other words, we decided that ST:TNG CCG should be a realistic simulation of the *Star Trek* series on which it is based.

This goal was achieved when we conceived the basic structure of the game using the spaceline—a row of cards which represents a sector of space and *locations* to which ships and personnel can be moved. They would have images of actual planets and space locations. By creating locations, we were then able to build upon them to fashion the desired realism. Ship cards would move back and forth along the spaceline. Personnel, equipment, etc., could be *loaded* aboard these ships and move with them.

Then, to create play which mirrored the interesting stories and plot twists seen in the 178 episodes of *Star Trek: The Next Generation*, we decided to make the spaceline locations double as "mission" locations. If you achieve the requirements listed on each mission card at that location, you score points, which in turn creates the basic objective of the game and how you win.

Finally, the key element of the game was the idea of Dilemma cards. If the game consisted of only moving personnel to mission locations, it would be too straightforward. Dilemma cards represent the unknown, and would literally be *hidden* from the players. They are plot twists which a person might encounter at a location. To simulate the unexpected *surprise factor* these hazards have in the show, they are hidden underneath the Mission cards at the start of the game by the players, so that you aren't sure what you might encounter at any one location. Thus, when you beam down to do a mission, you first have to get around any dilemmas that are there in your way—just as in *Star Trek*!

Of course, it took a lot of experimentation and playtesting before all the above ideas evolved. Even so, we hit upon this basic structure fairly quickly and our first solid playtest decks featured all these elements and remained essentially unchanged until the design was finalized.

Rollie, in particular, suggested and proved the value of several refinements aimed at streamlining the play and making it more efficient and more natural. One such revision was the concept of unlimited beamings for personnel on a turn, which greased the play and opened up an amazing amount of options and freedom for the players.

Darwin Bromley was brought in as a design partner, with an emphasis upon using his rare expertise as an avid collector, and as one of the few people who understood the arcane mathematical complexities of the randomization facets of CCGs. For example, one third of the cards are "common," one third "uncommon," and one third "rare;" in a ratio of about 11:3:1. The rarity of each card has subtle effects on the gameplay that have to be taken into account for the design as well, and Darwin was very helpful in this regard. Darwin made many useful suggestions on refining the game design from a collectible point of view.

A second goal for the design was a high degree of visual appeal and collectibility. All of the gameplay elements were shown to Darwin Bromley for feedback on how they would affect the appeal of the game to collectors, or how their charm could be enhanced. For example, at one point, feeling that we were short of room on the cards for icons and wordings, we thought about superimposing the name of the card across the photographic image, thus freeing some space. Darwin just about had a Targ on that one, and vetoed it!

Darwin, who was one of the top collectors and experts on *Magic: The Gathering*, and who has since designed several CCGs for Mayfair Games, also insisted that the design of ST:TNG CCG avoid the problem of trash cards. These are common cards which players only need a small amount of, and no more. Because they are common cards, people who collect sets end up with dozens, even hundreds of each one, which collectors found aggravating. We thus made it a third goal to design ST:TNG CCG to minimize this kind of technical problem, which included packaging, printing, and other design strategies.

The fourth design goal was that the game should be fun. This might seem obvious, but shouldn't go without saying. It would be easy to design a *Star Trek* CCG that looked good but played like "gagh." After all, lots of "licensed property" products like this tend to be poorly designed, counting on the famous name to create sales. But Decipher doesn't think that way, and besides, in this case the audience will be very critical and desirous of a game that plays well—not only as a nice simulation, but also as something with fun and surprise factor.

The final design goal was accuracy. It is no secret that *Star Trek* fans are among the most knowledgeable and eagle-eyed people in the Quadrant! We thus committed to ensuring that the facts listed on the cards were exact. But more than that, we wanted each card to realistically reflect the essence of what it was symbolizing, not only with the technical facts, but with its image and its very flavor.

Theme Limitations

As it turned out, this fifth design goal was the hardest to meet. As discussed earlier, designing the individual cards is the most difficult task, due to the matrix ramifications. ST:TNG CCG, however, had an additional complication—thematic limitations.

In any other CCG which is not based on a specific theme, when you need a card to have a certain desired gameplay effect, it is easy to simply dream up a name and a picture image for a card that fits that effect. In ST:TNG CCG, however, we had to remain true to the *Star Trek* theme. It isn't possible to "make up" something. Every card is taken directly from the series, using images or concepts exhibited in the series.

Thus, if you want to have a card which has effect X, you must find something which had a similar effect to X somewhere in the episodes—at least symbolically—which you can use as the image for that effect!

At first, this caused great difficulties for us. I don't know how many conversations we had that went like this:

Rollie: "We need a card that does (so and so)!"

Tom: "But there isn't anything in *Star Trek* that does that!"

As I got more into the depths of *Star Trek* and the subtleties of the game design, however, I discovered more and more ways to achieve the desired effects using the existing *Star Trek* images. The enormous conceptual depth of *Star Trek* has always provided an answer. As Decipher said in the ST:TNG CCG rulebook, "... thanks to the late Gene Roddenberry for creating such a wonderful universe in which to play."

Star Trek Canon

Canon, *n.* "A body of rules, principles, or standards accepted as axiomatic and universally binding, as in a field of study or art."

Star Trek fans, like me, have always enjoyed discussing and listing the "known facts" that have been revealed in the show. But to avoid argument, it was necessary to be strict about the difference between what is official and what isn't.

Official *Star Trek* info is rigidly defined. Nothing is considered to be real unless it has been used or explained in an episode. All the books, novels, lists, products, and other compilations of *Star Trek* information are not canon.

Paramount gave us this same hard-and-fast rule. We could only use canonical information that appeared in *Star Trek: The Next*

Generation. Since Paramount had the responsibility of approving every single card in the game, this meant we had to be able to justify every single fact and piece of information on the cards!

LCARS Anyone?

With this need for accurate and official information on hundreds of cards, the development phase of the product became extremely information intensive.

In fact, as Warren Holland and I discussed on more than one occasion, it was clear to us that a project of this information magnitude simply would not have been possible more than a few years ago. Not only are computers absolutely required to handle and process this information, but they must also have huge amounts of memory, as well as speed and video capabilities. We used over 1.5 gigabytes of information in developing just the initial set of cards—perhaps a drop in the bucket for the *U.S.S. Enterprise*'s LCARS computer, but impressive nevertheless. The entire project was done on computer, including all the artwork for the cards and their digitized images, which went straight from the computer to the printer. If the camera-ready artwork had to be done by hand, you could have added another eight months to the development time!

The Information Dilemma

Even so, the project chewed up time and pushed back deadlines at an incredible rate as we endeavored to nail down the exact wordings, images, and numbers on each card.

Part of the problem, paradoxically, was the lack of centralized information about *Star Trek*. With all the books and magazines and miscellaneous *Star Trek* info floating around, it was surprising to find that it had never been collected into one *single* official source.

Fortunately, we received some excellent help from *Star Trek* experts we contacted, like Larry Nemecek (author of *Star Trek: The Next Generation Companion*), and Bill Mason (Star Trek Club leader on America Online).

The dilemma was made worse when we realized that Paramount's library of slides and CD images were not sufficient in number or variety to meet our needs. For a few stardates there in the Spring of '94, the lack of official sources of information and acceptable images became a real dilemma for our mission. At one point, Decipher arranged to have Paramount haul their ship models out of prop storage for new photography to get the images we needed. This plan proved fruitless, anyway, as not all were available.

Luckily, two "interrupts" occurred to remedy the dilemma. First, in April 1994 the *Star Trek Encyclopedia* (by Michael Okuda, Denise Okuda, and Debbie Mirek) became available, and it proved to be just the kind of all-inclusive authentic source of information about *Star Trek* that we needed. Paramount was already using it as their own canon, and now so could we. It only covered the first 6 seasons of *The Next Generation*, but we could probably get by for the seventh season with alternative information sources.

Second, with Picard-like perspicacity, Warren Holland took the Targ by the quills and decided to solve the image problem himself. If the existing slide images were insufficient, the only alternative was to frame-capture the picture images from the shows themselves. We had been led to believe that this was not possible to do in sufficiently good quality.

However, Warren found that there had been some recent advancements in enhancement technology, which would allow us to enhance a digitized picture image up to higher quality. One company in particular had a new process that was wonderful! In the end, Decipher spent more than $40,000 enhancing the images on each of the 363 cards.

This approach also opened up the gameplay design. On video there are 30 frames per second in each episode, and every frame was potentially an image for a card, as opposed to being limited to only slides and special photography.

The process then became clear: Decipher secured from Paramount copies of every episode with "time codes" on the screen showing the exact frame number. Using an arsenal of Macintosh computers, we went through the episodes seeking the best image for each of the cards we wanted. I spent three weeks in Norfolk, 15 hours a day, slowly combing through the episodes in this manner (along with Ross Campbell, Warren Holland, and the other members of our video team). We pulled hundreds of reference frame captures for each show—over 6,000 images in all! The group then conferenced together, sifted through all these images, and selected the best ones for the desired card.

The criteria for what images we wanted were interesting, and the selection process came to feel like a mini-artform by itself. First, we wanted images that had never been seen before in magazines or in other *Star Trek* products. Second, we wanted images of higher quality than anything Paramount had available in their licensee library. And third, we wanted an image that was the quintessential image of that particular character—showing him or her in a setting that is appropriate to the essence of what that character was all about.

These goals made for subtle choices. We spent two hours one night just trying to decide between the last two images of Etana Jol, including bringing in no fewer that five other people for their opinion!

After these selections were made, Decipher had the same exact frames pulled from the original digital masters at Paramount. This digitized image then went through advanced enhancement. When Decipher's computer art department got its hands on them, they were further fine-tuned. Sometimes images were combined with prop shots which Decipher commissioned from Paramount. Images such as planets, which were only partly seen in the show, had to be created from scratch using reference images from frame pulls.

The images that resulted from this process are more than portraits of characters. They have a background to them that *Star Trek* fans can appreciate. For example, the picture of Lieutenant Commander Data is nicely expressive. It is from the episode, "The Offspring." It shows him just after he announced to the rest of the bridge crew that his daughter, Lal, had died. He then turns around and resumes work at his station with no outward show of emotion—except for the small glint of grief in his eyes. We felt this was the essence of his character in one picture—mechanical, with the human side visible underneath.

My personal favorite card image is Ro Laren. We wanted a card that showed her ambivalent, lonely character. This image, which presents her on the bed in a self-conscious pose with her shadow falling across the wall behind her projects this nicely. Other nice Personnel cards are Alexander Rozhenko and Reginald Barclay.

Make It Just So

With the solution to the information and image quality problems, the rest of the design came together nicely. But the process was still time consuming for the final step: committing to the exact word-ings on each card.

Not only does the effect of each card have to be explained correctly and clearly, but also concisely. Most of the cards only had room for three lines of written explanation, much less room than this paragraph.

Based upon playtesting feedback and last-minute insights, we were making subtle changes to the wordings of the cards right up to the very end. This included one memorable 14-hour long, 4-person, all-night conference call the day before the final art-work was absolutely due, arguing such galactic issues as whether or not to use italics on some key words as emphasis! Again, had it not been for the fact that the artwork was being done by computer, allowing for relatively easy last-minute changes, all of this would just not have been possible.

Of course, some cards, like the Borg Ship, are just too complex to explain in three short lines, and deciding what level of ambiguity we could live with was a constant issue. Fortunately, the existing knowledge people have of *Star Trek* means that ambiguities can usually be resolved with common sense until an official interpretation can be made— we took advantage of this in a few cases. Generally, however, it's amazing how much you can fit into three little lines!

Paramount's licensing department had the responsibility to approve every card. Ross Campbell at Decipher deftly handled this process, working with Guy Vardaman and Seema Molhatra, two of the *Star Trek* experts in Paramount's licensing department.

Vardaman has the interesting distinction of having appeared (as an extra) in more *Star Trek* roles than any other actor. Whenever they needed some background personnel, he would be there—as a Klingon, Federation, or Romulan; he wasn't choosy over the years.

Naturally, we wanted to make a Personnel card for one of these characters, and we did. You can see him as Federation Ensign Darian Wallace.

Vardaman also provided us with special details when needed. Most cards have a box containing background information of trivial interest which we call "lore." Sometimes little canonical information was available for a certain character or thing (particularly many of the Klingons). Vardaman created for us some *official* info to use on those cards. For example, Divok's card says, "Studied the effects of Tribbles on the Klingon nervous system." (This is, is as far as I know, the only official reference in *The Next Generation* about Tribbles!)

Vardaman and Paramount even allowed us to include new official data in the game. For example, the Federation Nebula-class ships have a holodeck! But you won't find this information anywhere else. We requested that Paramount let us have this ship attribute, arguing that they are comparable in size and age to Galaxy-class ships which have several holodecks. They agreed.

Paramount didn't always agree to such proposals, however. For example, in the original design of ST:TNG CCG, we had "starbases" instead of "outposts." We have a beautiful image of a Federation Starbase (from the episode *11001001*) that we wanted to use.

However, nowhere in TNG do we ever see a Romulan or a Klingon Starbase. Decipher offered to create realistic digital designs for these cards using known Romulan and Klingon architectural styles, but Paramount refused. The licensing department tries not to make decisions which may constrain the production department in the future.

Engage!

Originally we had hoped to have the game on the market in time for GenCon, the huge gaming convention that takes place in Milwaukee every August. But the various delays and the extra time needed to do the image enhancement, etc., conspired to make us miss that deadline by a wide margin.

We did have high-quality final mockups using the actual artwork on the cards at GenCon, however, which enabled us to get some pre-market feedback and promote the game at this event.

The cards are printed by Carta Mundi, the Belgian card manufacturer known for its quality and which helped pioneer the unique randomized packaging process that CCGs use. Luc Mertens, special project manager there, was instrumental in helping us navigate the nebulas of technical factors involved in printing and packaging this kind of game.

Due to the big demand for CCGs, Carta Mundi had by now been running an astounding backlog, despite their impressive printing facilities. So it was not until the first week of November that ST:TNG CCG finally hit the stores—just about a year since we first learned about the new genre of collectible card games.

Thanks to the power of *Star Trek*, the game was hotly anticipated, and the first three print runs were already sold out at a retail level before any of us had even seen the final product, so we were as anxious as anyone to see it! We were naturally very happy to hear the extremely positive reviews ST:TNG CCG received—from collectors, CCG fans, and *Star Trek* fans who knew nothing about CCGs.

Essentially, the only criticisms we received had to do with packaging, card mix, and misprint problems of various kinds. Decipher responded to these matters immediately, setting up customer service avenues on the Internet, and here in the real world.

Subspace

The folks at Wizards of the Coast told us they thought the Internet was a major factor in the success of *Magic: The Gathering*. Collectors use it as a very convenient method of trading and selling cards, while players use it as a forum to discuss the game and ask questions about the rules. We thought we were prepared to meet this challenge for ST:TNG CCG as well, but were still overwhelmed!

The Internet is the "subspace communications" of our day, allowing a wide variety of shortcuts to information, and it makes a perfect fit with an information-intensive product like ST:TNG CCG. We have set up dedicated computer services that anyone can access, containing the latest information, news, info, lists, pictures, and other cool stuff for the game. It also features sites for customer service, rules questions, trading, discussions, and so on. For a game company, the Internet provides a wonderful avenue of direct feedback from players who are not shy to tell you exactly what they think, with no sugar coating.

Decipher plans to expand upon this base with other innovative ideas for interactivity between players, collectors, distributors, and manufacturers. Their hope is to find systems in which everyone benefits from this synergy.

Looking to the Future

ST:TNG CCG was designed from the beginning to be expandable beyond the 363 cards that come in the initial set. The first expansion sets will aim at deepening the game further. Also, entirely new elements that we didn't have room for in the initial set, like Alternate Universe characters and Holodeck Adventures will be developed and featured.

Personally, I can't wait until I am able to defeat my opponent's killer Cardassian strategy with my all-Tribble deck!

Tom Braunlich

The Player's Guide

One of the exciting things about ST:TNG CCG is that there are so many aspects of the game, each with its own play elements and strategies.

There are at least four different arenas of strategy in ST:TNG CCG—four features of fun at which a fan can excel:

> **Customizing Your Deck**
>
> **Creating the Spaceline**
>
> **Playing the Game Itself**
>
> **Trading for the Cards you Want**

This section of the book discusses these aspects of the game in a series of related chapters written by Bill Muldowney. Of course, each of these subjects is deep enough for an entire book of its own. Thus, this guide provides a discussion of the basic fundamentals—plus some examples of particular tactics that you can use to begin your explorations of the game.

Remember one thing: The ST:TNG CCG universe is expanding... The game will evolve from its current form into deeper forms! Decipher Inc. plans many expansion sets, each with numerous cool new cards. As these new cards mix with the existing cards they will have exciting effects that ripple throughout the carefully created tactics you have discovered so far.

The expansion sets will not only have new cards with new strategies, but they will also have new cards which **change the strategies associated with earlier cards.** Some cards which appear strong now will become weakened. Some which appear weak now will become enhanced. Some of your favorite tactics will be made risky, while new opportunities for additional tactics will be opened for discovery!

Thus, as you read through these strategy tips, remember that they are only a guide and not eternal truth. Many of the general comments about the game will almost always apply, but particular comments and discussions of the uses of particular cards (such as in the "The 50 Most Powerful Cards" chapter) will change and evolve over time. Brady *GAMES* plans to publish new strategy guides with each major expansion of ST:TNG CCG, discussing the ramifications of each wave of new cards!

Just as in the real *Star Trek* universe, there are always new challenges! Only in a dynamic universe can you truly expand your power!

Customizing Effective Decks

As a Customizable Card Game, one of the interesting strategical elements of ST:TNG CCG is selecting the cards with which to play the next game.

There are as many ways to customize your deck as there are atoms in the universe! Your choices essentially reflect your personality—fans of the Klingons like to make decks concentrating on that affiliation only, and the same for those who like to run Romulans. Fans of the show often like to have a full Federation deck, with the entire bridge crew in play if they have them.

Some people like aggressive decks and often choose Klingon/Romulan combinations as a result—taking advantage of their cloaked ships and attacking advantages that the Federation lacks. Their goal is simply to wipe out the opponent, and then mop up in the scoring later. Often, they also rely on the use of lots of Interrupt and Event cards to harass the opponent.

Others take a defensive approach. They load their decks with an eye toward doing missions as fast as possible, and with defensive features to keep them alive long enough to do so! Others design decks on a whim. They play decks with themes, experimenting with ideas, or just designing them to create the maximum amount of storyline fun. Some like to use unbalanced decks (concentrating on a preponderance of one card, such as having lots of wormholes).

Then, of course, there are the people who seek to find the "ultimate" deck—one that is as unstoppable as a Borg Ship, taking advantage of loopholes they perceive in the rules, or cards which they believe are exceptionally strong. (Actually, we have been surprised that very few such decks have been discovered. Of course, when these secrets get out Decipher will undoubtedly come out with cards in future expansions to restore the balance.)

The point is that customizing a deck exhibits your personality—you can be serious or curious, aggressive or dutiful, *scurrilous or frivolous—it's up to you. Here are some fundamental deck-customizing concepts to get you started.*

In order to build an effective play deck, you should follow a plan that will maximize your chances of winning against any other deck you may encounter. If you plan your deck to beat Federation decks and then you come across a Romulan deck, you may be unpleasantly surprised with your results. By building your deck upon a solid strategy you'll have a deck that can play anyone and be competitive.

The following blueprint for deck building may help you to formulate some of your own deck ideas. The steps listed below are recommended for successful deck building:

1. Begin with Mission cards.
2. Choose personnel who can complete your missions.
3. Make sure you have Medical, Security, Leadership, and Engineering in your deck.
4. Add any Equipment cards to your deck.
5. Choose Ships.
6. Choose Event and Interrupt cards.
7. Select Dilemmas, Outposts, and Artifacts.

Begin with Mission Cards
(6 cards)

It's important to begin deck construction with your Mission cards since the object of the game is to complete missions and score points. By beginning with Mission cards, you'll have a better idea of what personnel and equipment you'll need to add to your deck.

One thing to keep in mind when choosing mission cards is that your opponent may be able to attempt *your* missions unless you choose missions he/she can't complete.

The overall strategy when choosing missions is to have as many of the six Mission cards you choose be missions that have *only* the affiliation symbol(s) of the affiliation(s) you are playing. For instance, if you are playing a Klingon deck, try to choose missions that have just the Klingon affiliation symbol on the bottom of the Mission card.

Another way to choose missions that are difficult for an opponent to complete is to choose missions that require obscure skills that few other affiliations have.

Choose personnel who can complete your missions
(10-20 cards)

Once your missions have been chosen, you need to select personnel who can successfully complete those missions you've chosen for your deck. At minimum, you should have two personnel in your play deck for each skill needed to complete a Mission card. By keeping at least two personnel in your deck for each mission completion requirement, you will increase the chances that you will be able to attempt missions throughout a game.

You can increase your chances further by doubling-up on key personnel. For example, if your missions involve a lot of Engineering, Computer Skill and Physics, then a card like Geordi LaForge is perfect as he has all those skills. It would be worth putting a second Geordi in your deck (if you have one) to insure he will come up early. Of course, here is where the "universal" personnel have an advantage. You can only have one Geordi in play at a time, so a second Geordi isn't really usable—whereas common Engineers like Gorta or Taurik can be used in multiples. If your strategy is long-term, two universal personnel might be better than two stronger non-universal personnel.

Balancing Personnel Classifications

(at least 1 card per category)

Put in a balance of the five most active classifications— Medical, Engineer, Security, Officer (or characters with Leadership), and Science. A quota of at least two of each is a good idea. (If you are using fewer personnel, including some Equipment cards which can provide these skills is smart.)

Although these skills may not be required to complete the missions you choose, they are valuable skills to have in any deck. Many dilemmas will require you to have one or more of these skills in your away team or on board your ship, so (whenever possible) try to insure your deck has at least one crewmember with each of these skills or add one of these skills through the use of equipment cards. Medical will protect your personnel on board or on the planets from diseases, plagues, and minor injuries. Engineering is necessary to protect your ship from any major catastrophes. Leadership (or any Officer) is necessary to engage in any combat whether between two opposing ships or two opposing away teams on a planet's surface.

Rollie Tesh calls the five most active classifications (Officer, Engineer, Medical, Science, and Security) the "Basic Contingency Group." Their skills cover most dilemmas, and if you are beaming down to attempt dilemmas missing any one of these classifications in the Away Team you are taking a risk. Civilians and V.I.P.s currently have less influence over these aspects of the game, although their uses will be developed in expansion sets.

You may also find that you want to have other skills in your deck. If you're constantly encountering Dilemmas or other cards that require a certain skill to be present, add that one to your deck. The process of deciding what cards are absolutely vital to your deck is an ongoing one. By replacing cards over time, playtesting the deck, and encountering various opponents, you will eventually have a deck that works well.

Add Equipment cards to your deck
(0-5 cards)

You might want to add Equipment cards to give personnel added abilities you feel are important for your deck. For example, an Away Team with 3 Officers +1 Medical Kit +1 Engineering Kit is essentially equivalent to an Away Team with 3 Officers +3 Medical +3 Engineer! If you are playing Klingons or Romulans, you might want to consider adding weapons to your deck to increase your Away Teams' attack capabilities. There are a lot of possibilities for adding equipment cards but, as with any cards you consider adding to your deck, make each choice carefully as you can only have a total of 60 cards in your deck!

Choose Ships
(3-7 cards)

The next step is to add ships to your deck. Depending on your overall deck strategy, you may want to add between 3 and 7 ships to your deck. If your deck is centered around completing missions as quickly as possible, then stay closer to 3 ships in your deck. You will likely get one out regularly, and you won't have too many ships and not enough personnel to run them. If you are playing a style that seeks to destroy the opponent's ships, then you may opt to put in more ships in an effort to swarm your opponent.

Regardless of the number of ships you choose for your deck, carefully assess each ship's relative strengths and weaknesses before finalizing your choices. Ships with higher ratings on shields, range, and weapons usually have a need for a greater crew skills in order to move them from your outpost. It may be useful to add a ship with a greater range but lower shields and weapons and use that ship primarily for transporting personnel to your main vessel.

You may want to consider a Husnock ship in your deck. This Nonaligned ship can offer excellent support to your main ship, and is also very good defensively (and has a holodeck to boot!). Also, with an unaligned commander at the helm, your Federation deck can gain some much needed offensive capabilities. The only drawback with the Husnock ship is range. Be sure to have other ships which have better movement if you want to be able to fully explore your part of the galaxy.

Choose Event and Interrupt cards

(5 cards)

Events and Interrupts are powerful cards. Some are hazards played on the opponent, while others are defenses to hazards. Still others are neutral—their use depends on how you combine them with other cards to creatively produce the effects you want. Each of these cards has its strengths. The key is to choose the right number of Events and Interrupts along with a strategy to complement your choices. It's at this point where the personality of your deck really begins to take shape!

Be careful when choosing Events and Interrupts. There are lots of attractive choices, and it's easy to load your deck with lots of Events and Interrupts. Keep in mind that for every card you add to your deck you must leave something else out to keep within the 60 card limit.

There are some Events and Interrupts that are *highly* recommended for any deck regardless of which affiliation you're playing. The following list indicates which cards should probably be used in any deck you make:

> Red Alert
> Res-Q or Palor Toff - Alien Trader
> Amanda Rogers
> Kevin Uxbridge
> Q2

You may find that you want to add more than one of some of the above cards to your 60 card deck. If you have a second of one of the above cards, you might try using it in your deck as well.

Select Dilemmas, Outposts, and Artifacts

(10-30 cards)

Dilemmas

Dilemmas are one of the most important cards you'll have in your deck. If you're able to choose dilemmas that will stop most of the opponents you encounter, your chances of winning will increase dramatically. The key is to strike a balance of Space Dilemmas, Planet Dilemmas, and dilemmas that can be both Planet and Space Dilemmas.

A good combination of dilemmas in your deck might be 4 planet dilemmas, 4 space dilemmas, and 4 dilemmas that are both Planet and Space dilemmas. This way, even if you encounter someone who's playing all space or all Planet Missions, you'll always be able to at least seed 8 dilemmas every time you play. You may choose more than one of the same dilemma (e.g. two Borg Ship space dilemmas), but you must seed the dilemmas at different mission locations on the spaceline.

(See the next chapter for more details about dilemmas.)

Outposts

Adding Outpost cards should be one of the easier steps to building your deck. You must have at least one outpost in your deck, and you seed that one outpost during the initial seed phase of the game. You may seed an additional outpost for each affiliation beyond one that you control. Beyond the outposts that you seed in the seed phase, you may also want to consider adding at least one additional outpost to your deck. Not only will that protect against someone destroying your outpost, but it may also provide a safe haven for your ships if you build one later in the game.

Artifacts

Artifacts are among the most powerful cards in the game. Each has special abilities. But to use an artifact in play one must first complete a mission where the artifact is located. This makes the player "earn" the extra power of the artifact.

Artifacts are seeded during the seed phase like dilemmas. Keep in mind that they can only be seeded at Planet Missions, so you need to insure you have some Planet Missions if you want to use a lot of artifacts.

It is wise to try to limit the number of artifacts in your deck to between 0 and 5, since often you never get them, and each time you add another artifact you must give up another card somewhere else. Also, note that it is possible for your opponent to acquire the artifacts you intended for yourself! If, for example, you try a strategy of placing lots of artifacts at an easy mission, you risk your opponent getting there first!

When selecting artifacts, make sure that the rest of your deck would complement the use of that artifact. For example, the Tox Uthat artifact, which allows Supernovas to be played, is useless unless you stock a couple Supernovas in your deck as well. (See "The 50 Most Powerful Cards" section for the detailed discussion of some key artifacts.)

Treaties and Multiple Affiliations

You should experiment with customizing decks that feature more than one affiliation. By combining affiliations, you combine strengths.

Among the advantages of having dual or triple affiliation decks are:

1. You get to start the game with more than one outpost, which provides you with more "safe" locations, more locations to attack from, and makes it easier to reach or dominate large sections of the spaceline. You are also less vulnerable to the strategy some players have of quickly attacking their opponent's outpost.

2. Your flexibility of doing missions is greatly increased.

3. Your ability to do your *opponent's* missions is also greatly increased. If you play all three affiliations, for example, you can do *any* mission! This is especially effective since often the opponent only stocks dilemmas to play against

your missions, and doesn't think to protect their own missions! They may have placed artifacts, for example, at their own missions, which you will have a good chance to get for yourself!

The disadvantages of multiple-affiliation approaches are:

1. To get full cooperation between your affiliations you need to utilize treaty cards, and thus you would need to stock at least one in your deck. Actually, you should stock more than one, to increase its chances of coming up early, and to have a backup in case your treaty is destroyed. Fortunately, the treaty cards were made immune to Kevin Uxbridge, but they can be destroyed by The Devil.

2. When you use multiple affiliations, there is a tendency to spread yourself thin across the gamut of your personnel. This can be disasterous if your treaty gets destroyed or if it takes a long time coming up due to bad luck with your card draws.

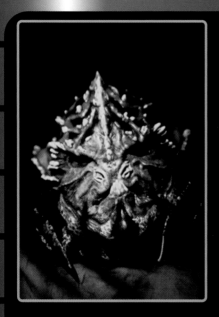

Strategies for Choosing Dilemmas

Dilemmas are the heart of the game, providing the unpredictable plots twists that crews must face, and through that the sense of suspense. Typically, players choose an array of dilemmas which they think will be particularly hazardous for the opponent, slowing him down or even preventing him from doing the missions around which he customized his deck. Thus, they have that "stab-in-the-back" factor that we all love so much!

Whatever dilemmas you choose to use in your deck, you should attempt to pair up dilemmas that work well with each other. By incorporating dilemmas that complement each other into your deck, you will be able to reduce your opponent's chances of victory. The following section will review dilemmas and will review some that work well together.

Space Dilemmas

TARELLIAN PLAGUE SHIP is a dilemma that's extremely valuable in a number of combinations. Since the card requires a person with Medical skills to beam over to the Tarellian ship (you discard the Medical personnel to your discard pile), it works very well with any other Space Dilemma that requires Medical skills to be overcome. You'll want to be sure to "seed" the Tarellian Plague Ship after any of the dilemmas which require Medical since dilemmas will be encountered in a last seeded, first encountered fashion.

Some of the other dilemmas that work well with the plague ship (and can be seeded on a space mission) are Menthar Booby Trap, REM Fatigue Hallucinations, Tsiolkovsky Infection, and Barclay's Protomorphosis Disease. The booby trap requires a Medical person to be present or one crew member is killed (random selection). By eliminating a person with Medical (through the plague ship), you will improve the chances of the booby trap being effective against your opponent.

REM FATIGUE HALLUCINATIONS kills the entire crew in three turns unless 3 Medical are present or the ship returns to an outpost. Combining this with the plague ship will almost ensure that the ship will now be heading back to an outpost (and you can attempt to delay that journey with Interrupts and Events like Q-Nets).

TSIOLKOVSKY INFECTION causes everyone onboard to lose their first listed skill until 3 Medical is onboard to cure the infection. The power of this card is evidenced by glancing at a handful of personnel cards. In most cases, the first-listed skill is the primary skill of any Federation, Klingon, or Romulan crewmember. Eliminating that first-listed skill will severely hamper any attempts at completing missions (or even keeping the ship functioning normally).

BARCLAY'S PROTOMORPHOSIS DISEASE kills an entire crew (except androids) unless Science, Medical, and Security are present. This dilemma also has a bonus of 10 points if the person encountering this dilemma is able to overcome it, so be aware that this one can backfire on you.

CRYSTALLINE ENTITY (Space/Planet Dilemma) kills all life onboard unless the shields are greater than 6 or Music is present. This dilemma also has a bonus point value of 5 points. This dilemma would only be useful against weaker ships and, therefore, may not be as valuable as some of the other Space Dilemmas you have for your deck. The advantage this card has is the fact that it has use as either a Space Dilemma or a Planet Dilemma. Putting this in your deck could be a good move if you consider that it can also be played on one of your missions, and you can collect the 5 bonus points on the card for having a ship with Shields >6 (or music).

ICONIAN COMPUTER WEAPON requires that non-personnel cards in hand are discarded and a similar number drawn from the top of the deck unless Science is present. This dilemma might fit in well with a strategy of having either you or your opponent run out of cards. If you can gain an early advantage in mission points, having either player run out of cards will result in a victory for you. This dilemma is also useful to force your opponent to discard some particularly nasty events, artifacts, equipment, or interrupts that he/she may have in hand.

BORG SHIP is certainly one of the most devastating dilemma cards in the game, and it also carries a bonus point total of 45 points (which is only gained if the Borg Ship is destroyed). Once the Borg Ship is in play, it attacks any and all ships in the same space. The Borg Ship has Weapons of 24 and Shields of 24 and moves one card at the end of every turn. This card is certainly valuable in just about any play deck. The thing to remember is that you may seed the Borg Ship under either your missions or your opponents'. If you seed it under your own, make sure that you either have an outpost at that mission, a Hugh card in your hand (which nullifies the borg ship attack for one turn), or some way of making your ship safe from the Borg.

NAGILUM is another Space Dilemma that can have devastating effects on your crew. This dilemma causes half of your crew (random selection, rounded down) to be killed unless 3 Diplomacy or Strength >40 are on board and has a bonus point value of 5. This card can be very effectively played against a Romulan deck, because Romulans generally don't have a lot of Diplomacy. It can be useful against any of the affiliations since 3 Diplomacy or Strength >40 can be difficult to achieve.

KTARIAN GAME is placed upon the ship encountering the dilemma and causes one crew member per turn (random selection) to become disabled. It can be cured with Cunning >30 (from non-disabled personnel only) or an android aboard. This would be more effective against Romulans and Klingons since the Federation player has a chance of getting Data or an Exocomp which increases the chances that Ktarian Game will not be effective. Since Romulans and Klingons have no androids in their affiliations, (without the use of special cards such as Lore's Fingernail), they will be more susceptible than the Federation. Romulans also have high Cunning, so Klingons are the most susceptible to the Ktarian Game.

BIRTH OF "JUNIOR" is a really good reason to make sure you have Engineering in your deck. This dilemma reduces range by 1 during each of your turns until 3 Engineering is present, and if Range =0 the ship is destroyed. This would be useful to play right before Cytherians since that card forces you to now move the length of the spaceline until reached. The Birth of "Junior" can severely reduce a ship's range making it susceptible to enemy vessels which might now swarm it. Junior is an example of unusual Dilemma cards which "enter play" once they are revealed. Most dilemmas have their effect and either are then discarded or remain as a block until they are overcome. Junior, the Radioactive Garbage Scow, and others, however, come into play almost like an Event card and remain in play until they are overcome. Junior attaches to the ship, and no longer is located at the Mission location where it is seeded. If the ship moves, Junior moves with it. Similarly, the Radioactive Garbage Scow must be towed away from a location before the mission can continue there.

CYTHERIANS, as mentioned previously, force the player to do nothing but travel to the far end of the spaceline with this ship and its crew, moving at normal speed, and not stopping even for Incoming Messages and battles. Completing this dilemma earns 15 points, but often causes the player to waste many moves. It is effective as a delaying tactic against the opponent. Plan to seed it underneath what appears to be a key mission for the opponent, especially ones that have high points (and which thus require lots of personnel to accomplish). Tend to seed it at missions near one end of the spaceline, so that the journey will be as long as possible. Finally, plan to have lots of delaying tactics cards in your deck, such as Q-Nets or Subspace Warp Rifts which can keep the ship busy, and thus out of play, for a long time. By the time he reaches the end and collects his 15 points the game might be over! When playing it upon your own missions, seed it near the middle of the spaceline to shorten the journey.

The Q dilemma, like Q himself, is one of the most powerful and unusual dilemmas in the set. (By the way, in the "Q-Continuum" expansion set, many additional Q-related cards will enter the ST:TNG CCG universe, possibly including additional Q dilemmas, too.)

This dilemma is an example of an "either/or" dilemma. If you can solve it, it helps you. If you can't, it helps your opponent. If you have 2 Leadership and Integrity >60, Q removes all the other dilemmas at this location for you! This is important, because this dilemma is effective to use against players who play massive-dilemma decks (loading up as many dilemmas as they can under your missions). Your strategy would then be to hold onto it during the seed phase for as long as possible, and then play it underneath a mission of yours which your opponent has loaded with dilemmas. It will thus be the first dilemma you meet when you eventually try to do the mission. Since you remember where you put Q (you will remember, won't you?), you will be sure you have the Leadership and Integrity to overcome the dilemma. Doing so will sidestep all those nasty dilemmas he has planned for you! (This is a general defense against any killer deck strategy that depends on large numbers of dilemmas. It also is a useful thing to keep in mind if you play any of the advanced variations of ST:TNG CCG which allow larger play decks and thus more dilemmas.)

Q also makes a good dilemma hazard—especially if your opponent likes to run a Romulan deck (who are low on Integrity). If using it against the opponent, play it early, so that if he happens to solve it there will be no more dilemmas left beyond it anyway. If the player fails to meet Q's requirements, the opponent gets to "rearrange the space-line." This includes rearranging each spaceline location, (and all the cards located under that location which move as a unit, such as the outposts and dilemmas), leaving the ships where they are. Rearranging can usually be done in such a way that the opponent is left in a horrible position, far from where he wants to be—just the kind of mischief Q likes!

NANITES, MICROBIOTIC COLONY, NULL SPACE, AND GRAVITIC MINE are all Space Dilemmas that cause a ship to be damaged unless the specific conditions on the dilemma card are met. Since any damaged ship that is damaged a second time before repairs is immediately destroyed, playing two (or more) of these dilemmas on a mission can be strategically useful. Each of the dilemmas require slightly different skills to overcome them, so that a ship encountering more than one of these dilemmas will have to be well staffed to avoid being damaged. It's likely that, if you damage your opponent's ship in this manner, he/she will head to the nearest outpost rather than take a chance on having a ship destroyed.

Planet Dilemmas

ARMUS - SKIN OF EVIL is a Planet Dilemma that is useful in just about any deck. The card states that one crew member (at random) is killed. There are only a couple ways to avoid this dilemma (an Interphase Generator being beamed down with the away team or a Genetronic Replicator in play and 2 Medical present in the away team). In any event, this is a powerful dilemma and one you should probably include in your deck if you have it.

FEMALE LOVE INTEREST, ANAPHASIC ORGANISM, AND MATRIARCHAL SOCIETY are three Planet Dilemmas that combine well in a deck. The Anaphasic Organism requires the female member in the Away Team with the highest total attribute numbers to resign (becomes discarded) unless

Security and Medical are present. The Female Love Interest card causes a female member (at random) to leave the Away Team mission and go to the farthest planet. Finally, the Matriarchal Society requires 2 females to be present to get past. The combination works very well as by the time the opponent gets to the Matriarchal Society dilemma, he/she will probably already have lost 2 female crew members to the other two dilemmas.

WIND DANCER is a very powerful Planet Dilemma card. It requires Lwaxana Troi or Music or Youth or Strength >9. At first glance that may seem like an easy dilemma to get by, but there are very few personnel who have Youth or Music and fewer still with Strength >9. Only Data, Worf (Federation), Fek'lhr, and Koral (Klingon) have Strength >9. Against the Romulans this can be a very nasty dilemma since they have no personnel above 9 in strength (of course Equipment cards may increase the strength of personnel). Romulans also do not have Music (Romulans aren't a very artistic group). Wind Dancer is definitely a strong choice for a Planet Dilemma in almost any deck.

ALIEN PARASITES is an "Anti Red Shirt" card. This strong dilemma is also a fun one, and works particularly well against players who like to use the controversial "Red Shirt" tactic of sending down small away teams to attempt dilemmas. If the opponent has a small away team (without Integrity >32), the parasites allow you to take control of his ship for awhile and do nasty things to it and the crew aboard. Even though it is still your opponent's turn, you are allowed now to control the ship and crew as you will until it is "stopped" (by running out of range, or engaging in battle, etc.). There are many creative ways to take advantage of this. You can play an Auto Destruct card on it, you can move it onto a Gaps in Normal Space card where it will be damaged. You can move it along the spaceline beaming off personnel as you go and stranding them on planets. You can move it to attack a Borg Ship where it will get crunched, etc. (If you do a mission with his crew, you get the points!) When the ship is stopped or you can't think of anything further to do, the opponent's turn resumes.

Thus, if your opponent likes to use the Red Shirt strategy, seed several of these cards. There are some other dilemmas that are tough on the Red Shirt strategy, and undoubtedly will be others in future expansion sets.

FIRESTORM is a dilemma card that will change. It is particularly effective against Romulans. It kills all personnel with Integrity <5, and the Romulans have by far the most of those. Furthermore, the only way to prevent this is if you have a Thermal Deflectors card—and Thermal Deflectors are not in this set! They were deviously planned from the beginning as coming out in the first expansion set. As a result, Romulan fans hate this card.

Actually, there is a story behind this situation. The designers wanted to make this card tough on Romulans, but did allow for a way out, with the plan to use the Emergency Transporter Armbands card to escape from the Firestorm. It seemed logical—you see the storm coming, you beam the hell out of there! The Armbands are an Interrupt Card which allow you to beam up/down personnel "at any time"—the designers thought it could be used to escape from the Firestorm dilemma as a result. However, this proved in practice to be a problem. Players started coming up with unintended ways of using the Armbands elsewhere to get around other dilemmas, in ways which were not intended and it became messy. Therefore, Decipher decided to rewrite both Firestorm and Emergency Transporter Armbands to be more specific—the "beta" set of ST:TNG CCG (Summer, 1995) will have those changes (along with fixes to some typos and a few other minor changes).

The new wording for these two cards will read as follows (and will be considered official for all editions of these cards):

Emergency Transporter Armbands changed "Beam Personnel up or down at any time, even during a battle before the winner is determined." to "Beam your Personnel up or down at any time, except during a dilemma (unless specifically permitted). May be used during battle before the winner is determined."

Firestorm changed "...unless thermal deflectors present. Discard dilemma." to "...unless thermal deflectors present or Away Team escapes using emergency transporter armbands. Discard dilemma."

This means the only dilemma which can be escaped from using the Armbands is the Firestorm, because it specifically says so. In future expansion sets, if there are other dilemmas which can be escaped this way, they will also say so. Note that if the Armbands are used, the Firestorm is discarded, but the Away Team was "stopped" by the Firestorm (since they didn't overcome the dilemma). Also note that the new Armbands card says "your personnel," rather than just "personnel," which was another problem with it because people were playing them on their opponent's personnel in outlandish ways!

CHALNOTH, REBEL ENCOUNTER, MICROVIRUS, ARCHER, EL-ADREL CREATURE are all dilemmas that will kill a single away team member unless certain conditions are met. Combining these cards at a Planet Mission can be a very effective way to eliminate one or more away team members. If you can eliminate that one vital member to the Away Team (the member who has a skill needed to complete the mission that no other away team member has), then you have effectively stopped your opponent from completing the mission and gaining any points.

IMPASSABLE DOOR AND HOLOGRAM RUSE both prevent the away team to continue until certain conditions are met. These can be valuable cards to have in your deck if you feel that an opponent would not have the necessary skills to pass. The nice thing about these dilemmas is that they don't go away until the requirement is met. A good strategy would be to put these dilemmas on Planet Missions at the far end of the spaceline. This way, if the away team can't pass, they'll likely have to travel a long distance to get someone with the necessary skill to pass.

Strategies for Well-Coordinated Decks

When it comes to the "play cards" in your deck (the cards which are not seeded, but which are drawn from the deck during play), it is wise to try to integrate your choices into a deck that follows an overall plan or theme.

This is a classic teamwork concept. You can have a lot of strong rare cards in your deck, but if they don't coordinate together well they won't necessarily be very effective. On the other hand, it is possible to make some very effective decks using just common and uncommon cards which coordinate well together, building upon each others' strengths.

The next two chapters discuss these strategies. This one talks about overall themes which your deck might take, using several examples. The following chapter details specific card combinations that are effective.

"No, you can't do that!"

It is always fun to frustrate the opponent, so a common deck strategy involves stocking lots of events and interrupts which are aimed at simply thwarting the opponent. The strategy would be to have cards in your deck that delay your opponent, stop his/her ships, and counter any cards he/she may play. Some cards that would help you to achieve these aims are Temporal Rift, any of the Incoming Message cards, Kevin Uxbridge, Amanda Rogers, Q2, Subspace Warp Rift, and a Q-Net.

TEMPORAL RIFT cards (Interrupt) can be played at any time and cause a ship to disappear for 2 full turns. This can be annoying to play on a ship which is loaded up with crew and ready to go and solve a mission.

The INCOMING MESSAGE cards (Interrupt) force a ship to return to the nearest outpost at full speed. This can be useful in stopping a ship from reaching a mission that is far from the nearest outpost. Once the ship approaches the outpost, the Incoming Message card would force it to immediately proceed back to the nearest outpost thereby prohibiting the crew from attempting the mission. A player may defend by having a Subspace Interference card, which prevents reception of Incoming Messages and other such things.

AMANDA ROGERS, KEVIN UXBRIDGE, Q2

This is an important trio of cards in ST:TNG CCG. They are an inter-related grouping of omnipotent beings, which can be used in positive or negative ways. To use them in a "You can't do that!" fashion, you stock plenty of them in your deck and use them to thwart the opponent's attempts to defend himself against your hazards by nullifying his defenses. Amanda Rogers nullifies any Interrupt just played (except Kevin Uxbridge or another Amanda). Thus, one example would be as follows: you play an Incoming Message on your opponent's ship, they try to block it using Subspace Interference, you nullify their defense by playing Amanda Rogers to nullify your opponent's Subspace Inteference, etc.

Similarly, Kevin Uxbridge nullifies an Event card (except Treaties). Since several Event cards are important defensively, you can try to wipe out his defenses with Kevin. Note that Kevin and Amanda are both pretty global in their effect, nullifying an entire class of cards, which thus makes them very flexible in use.

Q2's job is to nullify either Amanda Rogers or Kevin Uxbridge. If the opponent tries to nullify one of your nasty interrupts with an Amanda Rogers, you can play Q2 to try to nullify his nullification! Note that this can lead to a battle between these Q-Continuum characters—your opponent could then try to nullify your Q2 with another Amanda Rogers. If you have another Q2 you can nullify their second Amanda, etc. The last card in this chain wins this mini-battle of Qs!

Decipher plans a couple more variations on Amanda Rogers, Kevin Uxbridge, and Q2 cards in the future. These will be similar in function, but differing in the details in interesting ways. The "Two Player Introductory Game" version of ST:TNG CCG (a pre-customized set of two playable 60-card decks, available beginning in Summer 1995), contains two such cards—called "Countermanda" and "Kevin Uxbridge: Convergence." All variations on Amanda Rogers will be considered to be "Amanda Rogers" cards and the same for Kevin Uxbridge variations.

All of these cards are valuable in any play deck, but you'll need to experiment with how many of each you want to include in your deck.

SUBSPACE WARP RIFT cards (Event) are played across a space location and force any ship passing over it to either stop or incur damage. This can be a useful technique to slow down your opponent's ships. If your opponent has only played one or two ships in his/her deck, this may cause greater problems if you can then swarm and destroy the stopped ship(s).

A Q-NET (Event) can be useful to stop ships from crossing. A ship must have 2 Diplomacy onboard to cross the Q-Net. A good strategy here is to play with lots of Diplomacy in *your* deck so that you can cross your Q-Nets and your opponent is left stranded on the other side.

By adding cards like the ones mentioned to your deck, you'll see a theme when you play the game. The theme will be that your opponent will be stopped in various ways, his/her ships will be disappearing or head-ing back to outposts, and any attempts to play cards to overcome your strategy will often be overcome with your Amanda Rogers and Kevin Uxbridge cards.

"You can't win if you don't have cards."

Another strategical theme is to stock lots of cards which aim to cause your opponent to drain cards out of his/her hand or draw decks, making it difficult to plan. Draining cards from play means that the opponent's deck will go down rapidly, which in turn means that the maximum number of turns in the game can be half that of normal. Thus, a second aspect of this strategy can be to plan to grab a few points quickly, and then to keep this small lead long enough until your opponent's deck runs out, which ends the game. Some cards that take advantage of this strategy are:

KIVAS FAJO - COLLECTOR (Event) makes any player draw three cards from his/her draw deck. This card actually can be used in a variety of ways. One way is to allow you to draw three cards which increases your chances of getting a card you could really need at that point in the game. Another method is to force your opponent to draw three cards. This could be very useful if you are ahead on points and want to force your opponent to run out of cards.

THE TRAVELER: TRANSCENDENCE is played next to any player's draw deck. At the end of that person's turn, he/she draws an additional card from the draw deck. This could also be used to force your opponent out of cards or to give yourself more draw cards. Remember, whoever runs out of cards is unimportant, as the player with the most points wins regardless of who runs out of cards first. For this reason you may want to consider playing The Traveler: Transcendence on yourself more often than your opponent.

TELEPATHIC ALIEN KIDNAPPERS (Event) is another card with similar effects. This card allows you to guess a card type in your opponent's hand and, if correct, the opponent must discard the card. The real value, though, is that even if you guess incorrectly your opponent must reveal the card to you. Your chances of guessing the card type in subsequent turns increase dramatically. This card will have a tendency to paralyze your opponent because he/she will be limited in the number of cards in hand. Eventually, your opponent may only have one card in hand which greatly handcuffs the player.

THE STATIC WARP BUBBLE (Event) card is one that also paralyzes your opponent by limiting the amount of cards he/she can have in hand. Whenever you put this card into play, your opponent must discard a card before ending each of his/her turns. This will cripple your opponent very quickly and allow you to play cards since they will have trouble stopping you. The Static Warp

Bubble is powerful, although it can be destroyed not only by Kevin Uxbridge, but also by The Traveler: Transcendence—future cards will also come out that interact with it in surprising ways.

The deck that incorporates some or all of the above cards will certainly cause your opponent some difficulties and limit the responses they'll be able to make to your deck. You will find that, without a lot of cards in your opponent's hand, you will be able to act more quickly and gain a strategic advantage. Just be careful to make sure someone can't use this strategy on you.

"The Borg Deck"

Of all the adversaries the *U.S.S. Enterprise* faced, none were more fearsome than the Borg—a race of cybernetically enhanced humanoids who assimilated other cultures into their own, often easily. ST:TNG CCG includes several Borg elements into the game in the initial set, although this is just the beginning as there are plans to add much more Borg stuff in future expansion sets. You can build a deck theme around these cards.

In constructing a "Borg Deck," you'll want to incorporate many Rogue Borg Mercenaries (Interrupt), Crosis (Event), and Lore Returns (Event) as possible in your deck. The strategy will be to wipe out the crew on your opponent's ships while your own ship is off elsewhere completing missions.

ROGUE BORG MERCENARIES offer an advantage in that they can attack the crew of an opposing ship, and their strength increases with each Rogue Borg mercenary that is added. If I attack with three Rogue Borg, my total strength of attack is 9 (3 Rogue Borg of 3 strength each). If I increase that to 4 Borg, my attack Strength is now 16 (4 Borg at 4 strength apiece). Since the Rogue Borg Mercenaries card is an Interrupt card, you can hold as many of these in your hand as you choose and then play them all at once onto an opponent's ship.

CROSIS effectively doubles the strength of *all* Rogue Borg at a location and also counts as a Rogue Borg. So if a Crosis card is added in with 4 existing Rogue Borg Mercenary cards, each Borg is now worth 10 apiece for a total combined Strength of 50! Although Crosis' effects are not cumulative (each additional Crosis doesn't redouble the total), it is still wise to put more than one Crosis in your deck if you are planning a similar strategy.

LORE RETURNS is useful once your Rogue Borg Mercenaries have elminated the crew of a ship. Lore Returns allows you to now take command of the ship, move it, and even fire upon other vessels. This strategy can be very effective to eliminate your opponent's entire fleet.

The Borg theme can be an effective deck, but be aware of the fact that you still need to complete missions to score points and win the game. An effective Borg deck must be supplemented with enough skilled personnel to complete missions and score points. You should bear in mind that in order to win you don't need to score 100 points, but you do need to score more points than your opponent before one of you runs out of cards or is effectively eliminated from play.

"BaH" (Klingon for "Fire!")

A common and often effective theme is an attack-based deck. The goal is to hinder the opponent by brute force or intimidation. Your opponent can't do many missions if they're afraid to leave their outpost!

The obvious way to achieve this is by stocking lots of strong ships in your deck, bringing them into play, and staffing them with the minimum crew and a leader (so that they can battle effectively). Then, the ships are used in fleets which can destroy the opponent's ships. Of course, such a strategy works best for Klingon or Romulan (or both) affiliations, which have no attack limitations—and which also can utilize

based deck. The effects are powerful, and you may wipe out a ship and her entire crew this way if your opponent hasn't gotten out someone with the skill of Engineer yet.

The SUPERNOVA is, arguably, the most powerful event card in the game. By playing this card (though you must first have the Tox Uthat artifact in play before you can use this), you destroy everything at one mission location. If you are able to successfully play a Supernova card on your opponent's outpost, then the outpost and everything at the outpost are destroyed (ships, personnel, equipment, artifacts). Although this is a very powerful card, it requires a Tox Uthat be on the table first and that lessens the chances of you being able to actually use it. But a concerted strategy will sometimes be effective—seeding several Tox Uthats and stocking several Supernovas in your deck, as well as some Q2s to protect them both against Kevin Uxbridge.

PLASMA FIRE (Event) is played on a ship and damages that ship each turn until Security puts it out. This can be a way to cripple someone's ships and, combined with the other cards in this deck, provides a way to incapacitate the other player's ships and crew.

Powerful Card Combinations

Many cards may not seem paticularly powerful by themselves. But when combined with other cards in clever ways they can be very effective in a one-two punch. To some extent, card combinations can be planned for in advance, such as in the following examples. But often during play one must improvise with the cards in hand, creating clever combinations on the fly to overcome obstacles or to make difficulties for the opponent.

Here are some interesting combinations and strategies that you might incorporate into your deck.

Borg Ships and a Q-Net

This combination has many possibilities. You might put Borg Ships under your own missions and then use Hugh (Interrupt card) to nullify the Borg's attack. Once the Borg Ship is in play, put up a Q-Net somewhere along the spaceline and stop the Borg Ship at the Q-Net. (Borg Ships don't have Diplomacy and therefore cannot cross the Q-Net.) Now you can do a few things:

1. Wormhole your opponent's ships into the same space as the Borg Ship and the ships will be destroyed.

2. Wait until 2 (or more) Borg Ships are on the same spaceline and then use a Tox Uthat and a Supernova to destroy the Borg Ship and gain the 45 bonus points per Borg Ship.

3. Put the Q-Net up between 2 of your opponent's missions and then add Subspace Warp Rift (Event) to make it uncomfortable not to stop on that space. You may just want to leave the Borg Ship there since it will make it impossible to attempt that mission with the Borg Ship parked there and waiting to strike.

Cytherians or Incoming Message and Q-Net

This combination works well by making your opponent's ship have to travel to either the end of the spaceline (Cytherians) or the nearest outpost (Incoming Message) and then putting up a Q-Net to stop the ship from passing. Until 2 Diplomacy is aboard, the ship is stranded.

Cytherians or Incoming Message and Borg Ship

This time instead of stopping the ship, you'll have a Borg Ship heading at the ship from the opposite direction (the direction your opponent's ship *must* head in). If the opponent's ship can't cloak, it's in for some serious trouble.

Alien Parasites and Auto-Destruct

Once you've taken over the ship (the Alien Parasites dilemma), you simply use the Auto-Destruct card to blow it up. If you can move the ship close to another of your opponent's ships, it might do even greater damage taking out a second ship.

Betazoid Gift Box and Res-Q or Palor Toff

This is a combination that has proven overly powerful, so much so that there will be new cards coming out which are aimed at limiting it. The artifact Betazoid Gift Box allows you to pick three cards from your deck. Res-Q or Palor Toff are cards which allow you to regenerate a card from the discard pile. The basic strategy here, therefore, is to get the Gift Box, use it to pull three cards from your deck, including a Res-Q card, then use the Res-Q to get the Gift Box back again, reusing it over and over. This is a classic example of a powerful one-two punch.

In the initial set, there is no defense to this strategy except to try to block it using Amanda Rogers or Kevin Uxbridge, and it has thus proven to be too strong. (The tactic is limited under current official tournament rules.) It has been Decipher's policy from the beginning that whenever an overly-strong card combination is discovered, future cards will come out which inhibit that combination. The idea is not to simply prevent the possibility, but to instead take advantage of it to create fun effects, making the use of that strategy risky but still possible. The Countermanda card, which first will be seen in the Warp Pack giveaways, is one card aimed at this combination (and there will be others). If you have a deck strategy built around doing lots of Res-Q or Palor Toff regeneration of cards in your discard pile, you will be in trouble should the opponent have Countermanda.

Alien Probe and Telepathic Alien Kidnappers

This is a much-hated combination! In the current tournament rules, it is the only spe-cific combination that is banned (you can play each separately, but not at the same time). Telepathic Alien Kidnappers (T.A.K.) allows you to try to guess the card type in an opponent's hand and if correct force it to be discarded. Alien Probe forces both players to play with their hands exposed. If you play the two together, you can obvious-ly see what cards he has and easily guess correctly with the T.A.K., forcing him to discard one card per turn.

Again, future expansion set cards with provide more defenses as well as "in your face" ways to respond to this combination. In the meantime, many people play with a house rule against it, but it is fun to spring on somebody at least once.

Genetronic Replicator and Medical

If you have a Genetronic Replicator and at least 2 Medical present, your away teams are well protected from killer dilemmas. This is a great combination to play if you're playing planet missions.

Raise the Stakes and Kevin Uxbridge

This card certainly has gathered its share of controversy. It's a card that, when played, allows the winner of the game to randomly select a card from the loser's 60 card deck *unless* the opponent concedes immediately. Since the effects of this card are cumulative, each time Raise the Stakes is played the number of cards lost increases by one.

The idea is to have a Raise the Stakes and at least one Kevin Uxbridge card in your hand (and hopefully a lead in points). If the game goes well for you, there is no need for the Kevin Uxbridge card. If you start to lose, simply use Kevin Uxbridge to get rid of your Raise the Stakes card before you lose the game.

Metaphasic and Nutational Shields with a Klingon or Romulan Ship

The Klingon and Romulan ships can essentially attack at will if their shields are boosted by the Metaphasic or Nutational Shield cards. These cards boost the shields of all ships in play by the number of Science or Engineer aboard each ship. Although these cards can also be used to improve the defensive capabilities of a Federation starship, they are even more useful to give that Romulan Bird of Prey free reign of its part of the galaxy.

Bynars Weapon Enhancement, Metaphasic Shields, and Nutational Shields

These cards enhance the Weapons or the Shields of a Ship. Pumping up a ship's attributes that way can make them truly formidable. They are especially useful for Klingons and Romulans, who have the most aggressively oriented ships. Furthermore, combined with the right personnel you can get extra benefits. For example, Metaphasic Shields provide you with +2 on the ship's shields for *each* Science personnel aboard it, cumulative. If you plan an overall strategy which emphasizes having lots of Science, you could easily find yourself with several Scientists aboard the ship. Combining such a ship with Metaphasic shields would make it quite strong. For example, a ship with 3 Science and 2 Metaphasic Shields aboard would be +12 in shield power!

Trading Tactics

Whether you are a collector or a player, trading cards is part of the fun, and can even be profitable. You don't have to buy tons of cards to get enough cards to build a strong set. You can start with a minimum amount and trade for the cards you need to execute your own game plans. Here are some tips of the trade.

There are a number of trading strategies that you can use, but first you need to decide what cards you want and why you want them. Perhaps you want to trade so that you can complete the entire collection of ST:TNG CCG cards, or maybe you simply want to get B'Etor and Lursa for your Klingon deck. There are different approaches to take depending on what your ultimate objective is for collecting and trading.

Your best chance at getting some really good cards is to center in on one affiliation and get the rare cards from that affiliation. Due to the nature of the television show *Star Trek: The Next Generation* and the rarity of the cards in ST:TNG CCG, Federation personnel are likely to be extremely difficult to get unless you have a lot of cards to trade.

There are a number of sources available where you can find people who will trade with you.

Local Retailers

Many local retailers will either trade with you directly or may be able to direct you to a playgroup in the area that may have play-ers who'll trade. If the local store where you purchased ST:TNG CCG doesn't know of such a playgroup, try leaving your name and number with the retailer and perhaps you can start a playgroup in your town. You might also try local comic shops, card shops, and hobby shops to see if they know of any playgroups in your area.

Friends

Many of your friends may already be playing ST:TNG CCG but, if they're not, try getting a friend a starter deck as a gift. You can intro-duce him/her to a great game and also get a trading partner out of it.

Online Computer Networks

There are many groups on the popular online networks that have regular trading groups. If you have access to a computer and a modem, this can be a very good place to trade with another player. America Online, CompuServe, GEnie, PRODIGY, and most of the other online networks have a board that will list cards for trade and cards for sale. There are many places where trading takes place on the Internet. A good place to start is Decipher's own Internet site, decipher.com; which can direct you to such sites, including Decipher's ListServ mailing lists for traders/collectors. When trading via the Internet, take care to use standard techniques such as C.O.D. delivery or sending cards through third-parties.

Star Trek Conventions

There are *Star Trek* conventions every year all over the country, and the ST:TNG CCG has caught on well at these conventions. Not only will you learn more about the *Star Trek* universe, but you'll find lots of people with their cards ready to trade with you.

Making a fair trade

This isn't always easy to decide, but if the trade seems fair to you then at least it was a fair trade in your own mind. There are some basic guidelines such as card rarity, desirability of the card, and usefulness. Also, the black bordered Limited Edition cards are worth more than the white bordered cards.

As a general rule, if the two cards being traded have the same rarity, then the trade is "mathematically" fair. There is an equal number of rare cards available. That means that there are the same number of Jean-Luc Picard cards as

there are Cultural Observation cards, so mathematically it's a fair trade.

Getting the cards you want

One way is to look for collectors and trade with
them. Collectors are less concerned with how
powerful the card is and more with whether or
not they own the card. If a collector has a duplicate Data card and really needs a Cultural
Observation card, you might find that you're
able to get an even trade.

Look for collectors at gaming conventions
(such as GenCon, Origins, or the many
"cons" held in cities all over), or at *Star Trek*
conventions. They will provide you with a
good source for trades. Information about
some *Star Trek* conventions can be obtained
by contacting either of these sources:

Creation
411 North Central Suite 300
Glendale, California 91203
(818) 409-0960

Star Trek Fan Club
P.O. Box 111000
Aurora, CO 80042

Card Rarity

Although you can certainly decide what trade
you feel is fair, it is generally accepted that a rare
card for a rare card is a fair trade. Keep in mind
that a Jean-Luc Picard or an *Enterprise* may be
worth multiple rares because of the collector
value those cards have. (See the appendix for
detailed collectors info and stats on the cards.)

The 50 Most Powerful Cards

Almost every card (possibly even including Mot the Barber!) can be powerful at the right time or in combination with other key cards as we have seen. Yet there are many cards in the game which are considered always to pack a punch, even alone. Not all these cards are rare, by the way. Many are uncommon or even common, especially the ones which are often meant to be used in multiple like the Rogue Borg or Wormholes.

There are remedies and counter-strategies to every card, but here are 50 cards—plus "card #51" the exclusive Interrupt card available only through this book—selected and discussed by Bill Muldowney as particularly threatening.

ARTIFACT

STAR TREK
THE NEXT GENERATION

TM. © © 1994 PARAMOUNT PICTURES.

BETAZOID GIFT BOX

Traditional device for presenting important gifts. Its sculpted face comes to life boisterously presenting its contents to the recipient.

Immediately look through your draw deck for up to thirty seconds and choose three cards to place in your hand. Reshuffle draw deck and discard artifact.

Betazoid Gift Box

This can be a very powerful advantage and can easily shift the power of the game. If you have devastating cards in your deck (e.g., Supernova or Anti-Time Anomaly), being able to get them immediately might win the game for you (or at least cause your opponent some major headaches). As with all artifacts, place this at a mission you're fairly confident you can complete and equally sure your opponent will not complete.

The Gift Box allows you to look through your draw deck for up to thirty seconds and choose three cards to place in your hand. Before playing the Betazoid Gift Box, you should have a clear idea of what cards you are searching for (this requires a thorough knowledge of your deck) as you only have thirty seconds.

Look for cards that will hopefully turn the tide in your favor. Perhaps you'll want to get three personnel if you find that you need some key people to complete some missions. If there's a Borg Ship Dilemma card headed your way, you might opt for a Hugh card (nullifies the Borg attack for one turn) or a Temporal Rift card (ship disappears and reappears after two full turns). Maybe you need more ships in play and getting three ships out would be important. If you've got an entire handful of personnel and ship cards, perhaps a Red Alert card would be your best bet.

Whatever cards you choose, be clear on a purpose before starting to search and you'll be more effective in choosing correctly—and one step closer to victory.

ARTIFACT

STAR TREK
THE NEXT GENERATION

TM, ©, ℗ 1994 PARAMOUNT PICTURES.

HORGA'HN

Mysterious symbol of sexuality from the pleasure planet of Risa. To own one is to call forth its powers. To display one is to announce that the owner is seeking *jamaharon*.

Immediately play on table. Artifact allows you to take double turns from now on. (Not cumulative.)

Horga´hn

This is, arguably, the single most powerful card in the game. Having two turns to your opponent's one is often an advantage that your opponent simply cannot overcome. The idea is to get the Horga'hn early in the game and then take quick advantage of your opponent. Use your two turns to complete missions faster than your opponent and end the game easily.

Once the Horga'hn is in play, you need to make sure that you get ahead of your opponent by scoring more mission points. Since you're taking two turns to your opponent's one, you'll find that you will probably run out of cards much faster. Use this to your advantage by getting ahead quickly and then staying ahead.

An interesting combination with the Horga'hn is the Telepathic Alien Kidnappers card which allows you to guess a card type in your opponent's hand at the end of *each* turn and, if you're correct, the card must be discarded. You can cripple your opponent severely with this strategy as he/she will run out of options.

You'll find that taking two turns in a row will allow you to play more Event cards. Event cards have a way of really gaining you an advantage (mainly because they stay on the table and have lasting effects), so being able to possibly put two into play to your opponent's one can be a considerable advantage.

ARTIFACT

STAR TREK
THE NEXT GENERATION

TM, ©, ® 1994 PARAMOUNT PICURES

INTERPHASE GENERATOR

Experimental Romulan device that both cloaks and phases matter, allowing it to pass through normal matter.

Use as Equipment card. Nullifies: Chalnoths, Archers, Rebels, Impassable Doors, Phased Matter, Crystalline Entities, Armus, and Nausicaans.

Interphase Generator

This is considered an Equipment card and nullifies Chalnoths, Archers, Rebels, Impassable Doors, Crystalline Entities, Armus - Skin of Evil, and Nausicaans. Play this card with the Pegasus Search Mission card and lots of Planet Missions since the generator protects against most Planet Dilemmas.

One of the advantages of the Interphase Generator is the fact that it's an Equipment card. This means that it can be sent down to the planet's surface along with your away team. It can protect them from a variety of dilemmas which should make it easier to beam an away team down and have them return in one piece.

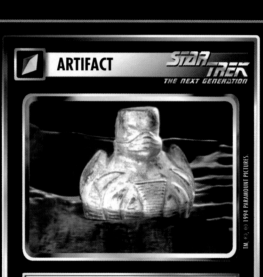

ARTIFACT

STAR TREK
THE NEXT GENERATION

TM, ®, © 1994 PARAMOUNT PICTURES.

KURLAN NAISKOS

Statues which open to reveal a multitude of similar but smaller figurines inside, representing the belief that each person is a community of individual voices and desires.

Place in hand until played on any ship as an Event card. If ship has all 7 personnel types aboard, its RANGE, WEAPONS and SHIELDS are all tripled. (Not cumulative.)

Kurlan Naiskos

This card can turn a ship into a devastating force capable of great range, weapons, and shields. It is played as an Event card on any ship and, if all seven personnel types (Officer, Engineer, Medical, Security, VIP, Civilian, and Science) are present triples the Range, Weapons, and Shields of the ship. If your deck has at least two of each of the seven types of personnel on board, you may want to consider adding the Kurlan Naiskos to your deck.

Once you get Kurlan Naiskos on one of your ships, you'll be able to track down and attack your opponent's ships. Since your range is tripled, even a normally slow ship will easily catch the fastest ship in the galaxy. This artifact is especially useful in a Klingon or Romulan deck since they can attack at will. In a Federation deck, the advanced speed and shields will make it much easier to get to various missions unscathed.

ARTIFACT

STAR TREK
THE NEXT GENERATION

TM, ©, ℗ 1994 PARAMOUNT PICTURES.

THOUGHT MAKER

Outlawed Ferengi mind control device. Transmits signals that implant sensory experiences and triggers emotions and memories.

Place in hand until played once as an Interrupt card. Look at opponent's draw deck for ten seconds and rearrange as desired.

Thought Maker

This Ferengi mind control device, once used on Jean-Luc Picard, is a powerful strategic card. Played as an Interrupt, it allows you to look at your opponent's draw deck for ten seconds and rearrange as you choose. If played at the right time, this card may insure your victory!

Once you've solved the Planet Mission where the Thought Maker is hidden, you may place the artifact in your hand. It may now be played at any time since it's an Interrupt card. The key to playing this card is in waiting for the right opportunity in the game.

Let's say your opponent has one ship in play and only a handful of Personnel cards in play. You can play the Thought Maker, take all Personnel cards in his/her draw deck, and then place them on the bottom of the deck. This will make it very difficult for your opponent to complete missions, battle your away teams, or do much of anything.

Another strategy is to quickly locate all your opponent's ships and place them at the bottom of the deck. If your opponent has not managed to get a ship in play yet, this will be totally devastating. Unless your opponent can somehow find a way to get those ships into play, you will certainly win.

The key is to know what to look for (quickly!), find the cards, and place them on the bottom in ten seconds or less. If you have an idea of what you need to get out of play before playing the Thought Maker, you will stand a good chance of being able to achieve your strategy.

ARTIFACT

STAR TREK
THE NEXT GENERATION

TM, ©, © 1994 PARAMOUNT PICTURES.

TIME TRAVEL POD

Craft from the future, stolen in the past by Berlinghoff Rasmussen for his own gain.

Place in hand until played once as an Interrupt card on any ship. That ship travels into the future (disappears for up to 5 turns). Pre-announce the return time.

Time Travel Pod

You might play this on your own ship to avoid the Borg Ship or any other problem you may encounter. As a weapon against an opponent, it can be used to delay a ship for up to five turns. Since the Time Travel Pod is discarded after use, it can be brought back to your hand using a Res-Q or Palor Toff—Alien Trader card. (See also page 81.) This can be a useful card to postpone your opponent from attempting missions. The strategy is to wait until his/her ship is about ready to attempt a mission and then force the ship to travel into the future.

This can be one of the most frustrating cards in the game if played at the right moment. Since it's played as an Interrupt, you can play it at any time on either your turn or your opponent's. The key is to wait until a moment when the card will have the most usefulness. Late in the game might be the perfect time to stop your opponent's flagship from attempting the mission, or maybe you'll decide to play it right after a Cytherians Dilemma card has been found. This one can be fun, but it's another card that will really frustrate your opponents.

ARTIFACT

STAR TREK
THE NEXT GENERATION

TM, ©, ℗ 1994 PARAMOUNT PICTURES.

TOX UTHAT

Dangerous quantum phase inhibitor invented in the future by Kal Dano who hid it in the 22nd century for safekeeping.

Place in hand until played on table as an event (supernova can be played on later turn) OR as an interrupt (prevents supernova). Discard after use.

Tox Uthat

When played as an Event card and then used with a Supernova, it can devastate the opponent and lead to a winning position for you. It can also be used as an Interrupt card to prevent someone using a Supernova card on you. The Tox Uthat/Supernova combination destroys all life, artifacts, ships, equipment, outposts, dilemmas, and planets at a single spaceline location!

This card is one that doesn't need a lot of thought to see how strategically useful it can be. Destroying your opponent's only outpost can win the game automatically if all of his/her ships are at the outpost when it's destroyed. A good strategy with Tox Uthat is to also put the Betazoid Gift Box at the same planet location—you'll be able to go through your deck, get your Supernova card, and wreak havoc on your opponent next turn.

ARTIFACT

STAR TREK
THE NEXT GENERATION

TM, ® , © 1994 PARAMOUNT PICTURES.

VARON-T DISRUPTOR

Only five of these pistols were made before being banned by the Federation. These vicious weapons disrupt the body from the inside out, causing a slow and painful death.

Use as Equipment card. Doubles all of your personnel's STRENGTH where present. (Not cumulative.)

Varon-T
Disruptor

This powerful artifact, banned by the Federation, is a powerful offensive (and defensive) weapon. Where the Varon-T is present, all your personnel have their Strength doubled. As an offensive weapon, you might use it with a Romulan or Klingon away team sent to wreak havoc on opposing planet forces. On the other hand, it might be used by a Federation away team to dissuade Klingon or Romulans from attacking.

As with all artifacts, place the Varon-T Disruptor under a Planet Mission during the initial seed phase. Once you have successfully completed the mission, you may play the Varon-T Disruptor as an Equipment card. It's important to realize that it's an Equipment card, as you may be able to play it immediately once you've completed a mission (especially if a Red Alert is in play).

Keep the Varon-T Disruptor on your ship and it will also help in fighting off any Rogue Borg Mercenaries that might try to take over your ship. A crew with doubled Strength will usually be more than a match for the Rogue Borg. (Unless a card in a future expansion set changes that.) It can also be effective in dealing with dilemmas, Events, or Interrupts that have Strength numbers as a requirement.

ARTIFACT

STAR TREK
THE NEXT GENERATION

TM, ®, © 1994 PARAMOUNT PICTURES.

VULCAN STONE OF GOL

Ancient Vulcan telepathic weapon. Kills by magnifying aggressive and violent thoughts, but can be blocked by peaceful thoughts.

Place in hand until played as an Event card.
Kills everyone in an Away Team without Youth
OR CUNNING>7. Discard artifact.

Vulcan Stone of Gol

This ancient Vulcan weapon, capable of destroying virtually an entire away team, can be an extremely valuable strategic card. Klingons and Romulan away teams will be slightly more susceptible to this artifact as their Cunning ratings are often not above 7, and there aren't many personnel with Youth in their ranks.

The strategy with this card is to place it under one of your Planet Missions during the initial seed phase, and then uncover it (by completing the mission). After you have the Vulcan Stone of Gol in your hand, you can play it as an Event card during one of your turns.

The secret for effective use of this artifact is to stop your opponent's away team so that you can play the Vulcan Stone of Gol on your next turn. This is most effectively done by choosing Planet Dilemmas that will allow you to stop your opponent (see the chapter called "Customizing Effective Decks" for more information on choosing dilemmas).

DILEMMA

STAR TREK
THE NEXT GENERATION

TM, ®, © 1994 PARAMOUNT PICTURES

ARMUS — SKIN OF EVIL

Malevolent being formed when the inhabitants of
Vagra II rid themselves of all the evil they have inside.

Kills one Away Team member (random selection).
Discard dilemma.

Armus - Skin of Evil

This is a Planet Dilemma that is useful in just about any deck. There are only a couple of ways to avoid this dilemma (an Interphase Generator being beamed down with the Away Team or a Genetronic Replicator in play and 2 Medical present in the Away Team). In order to maximize the effect of Armus, you can play Kevin Uxbridge in your deck (to eliminate Genetronic Replicators).

Since Armus – Skin of Evil kills one away team member at random, it's important to make sure that this is the first dilemma encountered by your opponent (which means you'd seed it last). The reason for this is that other dilemmas may require certain types of personnel to be present in order to overcome the dilemma, so eliminating a crew member early in the mission will make it even more difficult to complete the rest of the mission.

DILEMMA

STAR TREK
THE NEXT GENERATION

TM, ©, © 1994 PARAMOUNT PICTURES.

BARCLAY'S PROTOMORPHOSIS DISEASE

Contagious affliction which causes animals to de-evolve into ancestral forms. Disease named for Lieutenant Reginald Barclay.

Entire crew or Away Team (except androids) de-evolves (dies) unless MEDICAL, SCIENCE and SECURITY present. Discard dilemma.

10

Barclay's Protomorphosis Disease

Barclay's Photomorphosis Disease, named for Lieutenant Reginald Barclay, had some devastating effects on the crew of the *Enterprise*. Everyone onboard (except for Data and Picard) de-evolved into a more primal version from their ancestry. In ST:TNG CCG the card representing this disease is equally devastating. Unless Medical, Science, and Security are present, an entire away team or crew dies.

This is an advantageous card to play in your deck since it can be placed on either Space or Planet Missions. This way your strategy is not determined by your opponent, and you can place this card in your deck knowing you'll be able to seed it somewhere on the spaceline.

One different strategy with this card is to place it under one of your own missions. Overcoming this dilemma has a bonus of 10 points, and you could make sure you have the required personnel on board (or in your away team) and collect the 10 points.

DILEMMA

★★★★ STAR TREK
THE NEXT GENERATION

TM, ®, © 1994 PARAMOUNT PICTURES

BORG SHIP

Gigantic cubic ship of the Borg collective. Possesses powerful weapons and remarkable regenerative abilities.

Self-controlling ship (WEAPONS=24, SHIELDS=24). Start here. Attacks everything. End of every turn, moves 1 card toward and off spaceline's long end. Destroy for bonus.

45

Borg Ship

The Borg collective is perhaps the most feared of any of the Federation's enemies. The Borg know no allies and assimilate everything of value in their path into the collective. Their weapons and shields have no equal in the Federation, Klingon, or Romulan affiliations. The Borg are relentless—moving slowly, but persistently, across the galaxy.

In the game, the Borg Ship moves one card toward the far side of the spaceline. It attacks every and any ship in its path with Weapons of 24. Although there is a 45 point bonus for destroying a Borg Ship, not many will venture into its path.

There are a number of strategies with the Borg Ship Dilemma. One strategy is to use a Wormhole to place the Borg Ship in the same space as one of your opponent's ships. The Borg Ship will now attack your opponent's ships and likely destroy it. You can use a Q-Net to fence in one or two of the Borg Ships. Once the ships are stopped, you can use a Supernova (with a Tox Uthat) to destroy that space and both Borg Ships. You can also play an Incoming Message card and force your opponent to head directly into the path of the Borg.

There are some strategies to handle the Borg Ship. If you are playing Klingons or Romulans, you can cloak at the end of your turn which will likely keep you safe from the oncoming Borg. Other strategies are to keep a Hugh card in your hand. Hugh can nullify the attack of either Rogue Borg Mercenaries or the Borg Ship. The Borg Ship has many other creative uses, some of which can backfire on you if the opponent is prepared. It will be enhanced further in upcoming expanshion sets.

DILEMMA

STAR TREK THE NEXT GENERATION

TM, ©, © 1994 PARAMOUNT PICTURES.

CYTHERIANS

Race which explores the galaxy by giving other species the temporary ability and strong compulsion to come to them.

Place on ship. Ship must do nothing but travel to far end of spaceline at normal speed. When reached, discard dilemma. Score points.

15

Cytherians

The Cytherians are a powerful alien race who have the capacity to draw others to them—even from far across the galaxy. If this Space Dilemma is uncovered while attempting a mission, it is placed on the ship. That ship must do nothing but travel to the far end of the spaceline (at normal speed only). Once the end of the spaceline is reached, the controller of the ship gets 15 points toward victory.

There are (at least) two strategies which can be used with the Cytherians dilemma. One is to use it against your opponent and seed the Cytherians at a Space Mission as far toward one end of the spaceline as possible. Once your opponent starts toward the other end of the spaceline, you can play cards that slow, stop, or make the journey difficult. A Q-Net, Wormhole, Temporal Rift, Time Travel Pod, Tetryon Field, or Subspace Warp Rift are all cards that will make the ship's journey difficult.

The other basic strategy with the Cytherians dilemma is to play it on *your* missions. The 15 bonus points you can gain for reaching the end of the spaceline may be just the advantage you need to score a victory over your opponent. A useful card to play here would be Where No One Has Gone Before. This would allow you to leave the end of the spaceline and reach the other end much quicker than having to travel the entire length.

DILEMMA

★ST★R TREK
THE NEXT GENERATION

NAGILUM

Extra-dimensional entity willing to kill in order to understand the concept of mortality.

Half of crew is killed (random selection, round down) unless 3 Diplomacy OR STRENGTH>40 aboard. Discard dilemma.

5

TM, ® & © 1994 PARAMOUNT PICTURES.

Nagilum

This card can be very effectively played against a Romulan deck, because Romulans generally don't have a lot of Diplomacy. It can be useful against any of the affiliations since 3 Diplomacy or Strength >40 can be difficult to achieve. Use this card to delay your opponent from completing a mission. Seeded last, this card will often force an opponent to get reinforcements before being able to proceed.

DILEMMA

STAR TREK
THE NEXT GENERATION

TM, ©, © 1994 PARAMOUNT PICTURES.

Q

Incorrigible, extra-dimensional member of the Q Continuum, a race of omnipotent beings. Q exhibits a child-like petulance and sense of playfulness.

If 2 Leadership and INTEGRITY>60, discard all dilemmas here. Otherwise, Q allows opponent to rearrange spaceline locations. Discard dilemma.

Q

Q is, most likely, the most powerful adversary the *Enterprise* has ever faced. Although he is extremely powerful and capable of destroying the *Enterprise* and its crew with a thought, Q has shown more of a curiosity with the crew, particularly Jean-Luc Picard. In the ST:TNG CCG, the Q dilemma exhibits the same playfulness as the character Q in the series. If the opponent uncovers the Q dilemma, unless your opponent has 2 Leadership and Integrity >60 you get to rearrange the spaceline any way you so choose. If your opponent does have the requirements, then all other dilemmas here are discarded.

The first strategy, which may be fairly obvious, is to seed the Q dilemma on one of your opponent's missions. In this way your opponent will encounter the Q dilemma last so that, even if he does have 2 Leadership and Integrity >60, there will be no more dilemmas to be discarded.

The other strategy, relative to seeding the Q dilemma, may not be quite as obvious. You can seed the Q dilemma on one of your own missions. The idea is that you'll be able to discard all the dilemmas that your opponent has placed on your mission and then easily complete the mission. Of course, you'll need to not only have the required skills and attributes to overcome Q, but you'll want to try and make sure you seed Q last (so you'll be able to encounter him first when you attempt your mission).

DILEMMA

STAR TREK
THE NEXT GENERATION

TM, ®, © 1994 PARAMOUNT PICTURES

TARELLIAN PLAGUE SHIP

Ship containing the survivors of a Tarellia war plague. Infected from biological weapons, they are now refused entry everywhere.

All ship's crew immediately die from plague unless MEDICAL volunteers to permanently beam over (discarded) to Tarellians. Discard dilemma.

5

Tarellian Plague Ship

This Dilemma card works very well with any other Space Dilemma that requires Medical to be overcome. Some of the other dilemmas that work well with this card (and can be seeded on a Space Mission) are Menthar Booby Trap, REM Fatigue Hallucinations, Tsiolkovsky Infection, and Barclay's Protomorphosis Disease. Playing any of these dilemmas along with the Tarellian Plague Ship will be effective against your opponents.

Since Medical is a much needed skill, being able to eliminate a crew member with that skill can be a big strategic advantage. Even if you don't happen to have some of the dilemmas that require Medical to be overcome at this mission, future missions that your opponent attempts may require the Medical skill. Of course, if the opponent has taken the risk of exploring with no Medical aboard, he will pay a heavy price.

Note that Medical skill that comes from the use of Equipment cards like the Medical Kit can also be used to save the crew from the plague.

DILEMMA

TSIOLKOVSKY INFECTION

Variety of water-based Psi 2000 virus. Passed by perspiration. Creates dangerous intoxication-like instability among a crew.

Place aboard ship. It is now infected. Mission can continue but all personnel, while aboard, lose their first-listed skill. Cure with 3 MEDICAL to discard.

Tsiolkovsky Infection

The Tsiolkovsky Infection Dilemma card causes instability to anyone who becomes affected by the disease. Since the infection is so easy to contract (it spreads from perspiration), virtually all the members of a crew will very shortly be affected unless there is a lot of medical treatment. In the ST:TNG CCG, everyone on the ship is infected and loses their first listed skill while aboard. If there is 3 Medical aboard the infection is cured (and the Tsiolkovsky Infection card is then discarded).

You can combine Tsiolkovsky Infection and Tarellian Plague Ship underneath one of your opponent's Space Missions. make sure that the Tsiolkovsky Infection is seeded before the Tarellian Plague Ship so that the Medical must be sent to the Tarellians before the infection comes aboard. The chances of your opponent having an additional 3 Medical onboard is slim to none.

You might also use a Thought Maker (allows you to rearrange your opponent's draw deck) and put all his/her personnel that have Medical on the bottom of the draw deck. Then, when your opponent encounters the Tsiolkovsky Infection, there will be little that can be done to combat it.

DILEMMA

STAR TREK
THE NEXT GENERATION

TM, ®, © 1994 PARAMOUNT PICTURES

WIND DANCER

Sentry of the Parallax Colony. Only allows those whose hearts are joyous to pass.

To get past, Lwaxana Troi must be present OR at least one Away Team member must have: Youth OR Music OR STRENGTH>9.

Wind Dancer

Wind Dancer only allows the joyous of heart to pass his post and, in the case of the game, that means you need Youth or Music or Lwaxana Troi or Strength >9 to pass. (Strength >9 is allowed here because Lieutenant Worf got past it on the show with a punch to the jaw!) This type of "blocker" is effective since your opponent must stop and come back later with the appropriate personnel to attempt this mission.

The Romulans will have a particularly tough time with this dilemma since they have no personnel with Strength >9 and no one with Music ability. Of course, none of the affiliations will have an easy time with Wind Dancer which makes it a good Planet Dilemma in anyone's deck.

EVENT

*STAR TREK
THE NEXT GENERATION*

TM, ® © 1994 PARAMOUNT PICTURES.

ANTI-TIME ANOMALY

Q-created phenomena. Rift caused by anti-time particles in the future. Anomaly grows backward in time endangering all life in the past.

Plays on table. Kills literally ALL personnel on table (both players' cards) at the end of your third full turn, unless anti-time anomaly destroyed first.

Anti-Time Anomaly

In the final episode of the series, an anti-time anomaly almost destroys all humanity (as Q looks on). If not for Jean-Luc Picard and the rest of the crew of the *Enterprise*, perhaps all life would have been destroyed. Bring this card into play as an Event card and, at the end of your third full turn, *all* personnel in play on the table are killed (discarded) unless the Anti-Time Anomaly is destroyed first.

If your opponent has more personnel in play, you might want to consider playing this card and wiping out all Personnel cards in play. This way you can then equal the odds a little.

Another idea is to hold the Anti-Time Anomaly in your hand and allow your opponent to keep playing Personnel cards while you hold off playing yours. Once you get a Red Alert! card in your hand (along with a number of personnel), you can play the Anti-Time Anomaly, wipe out all your opponent's personnel, and then play your Red Alert! the next turn. The Red Alert! will allow you to now play *all* your personnel. Of course this strategy takes patience, and you may want to have cards in your hand to stop your opponent from destroying your Anti-Time Anomaly before your third full turn ends.

EVENT

STAR TREK
THE NEXT GENERATION

TM, ®, © 1994 PARAMOUNT PICTURES

GENETRONIC REPLICATOR

Medical device invented by Dr. Toby Russell. Capable of growing replacements for damaged organs.

Plays on table. Prevents any of your Away Team members from being killed if 2 MEDICAL present.

Genetronic Replicator

This card is valuable, especially if you plan a lot of planet missions. If you have 2 Medical personnel present in the Away Team, it can prevent personnel from being killed by nasty dilemmas like Armus – Skin of Evil, or the Nausicaans, etc. (by healing the affected personnel, as it did when used on Lieutenant Worf).

Note that when it says it requires 2 Medical present, this means two Medical personnel who are *unaffected* by whatever it is that attacks the Away Team. (Which makes sense, you must have two healthy doctors to run the medical equipment. The patient can't also be one of the doctors!) For example, if you Away Team with 2 Medical present uncovers the Armus – Skin of Evil dilemma, one person will be selected randomly to be "killed." This person will instead be "saved" by the Genetronic Replicator. However, if the selected person was one of the two Medical personnel, he/she will not be saved, because there was only on unaffected Medical present to utilize the Replicator. Similarly, dilemmas which are capable of "killing the entire Away Team" will overcome the use of the Genetronic Replicator since all the Medical present will be affected (i.e., no uninjured personnel are left to run the Replicator).

When using the Genetronic Replicator, stock at least 4 Medical in your deck, and also consider a Medical Kit or two to help beef up your Medical presence. When in play, your Away Teams are relatively well protected. Just remember that the Replicator only protects Away Team members and not crew on your ship.

EVENT ★ *STAR TREK THE NEXT GENERATION*

TM ℗ & © 1994 PARAMOUNT PICTURES

HOLO-PROJECTORS

The hologram projector on Minos is an example of planet-based interactive holographic technology.

Plays on table. This technology allows your holographic re-creations to be projected and used on any of your ships or Away Teams. (Immune to Kevin Uxbridge.)

Holo-Projectors

Each of the affiliations (Klingon, Romulan, and Federation) have at least one holographic Personnel card. The Holo-Projectors allow you to beam these personnel to the planet's surface and attempt missions. Furthermore, unless your ship has a Holodeck, you can't normally use holographic personnel for Space Missions. When you have a Holo-Projectors card in play, you may now use these personnel for Space Missions and Planet Missions.

Although this may not seem like a major advantage in and of itself, there is one important quality to holographic personnel that makes this desirable.

Holographic personnel, since they aren't alive, cannot be killed. You can beam a holographic member of your crew to the planet's surface (provided you have a Holo-Projector) and use him/her to explore the planet. In this way, you get a chance to see what awaits you on the surface before beaming any "live" personnel to the surface. Of course, such a strategy can be risky if certain "anti-red shirt" dilemma cards are encountered, see pages 60-61.

Note that Holo-Projectors are not vulnerable to Kevin Uxbridge, who normally could destroy Event cards. Future ST:TNG CCG expansion sets will expand the number of holographic personnel in the game—thereby making the Holo-Projectors an even more useful (and valuable) card.

EVENT

STAR TREK
THE NEXT GENERATION

TM, ©, ® 1994 PARAMOUNT PICTURES.

KIVAS FAJO — COLLECTOR

Treacherous collector of rare one-of-a-kind antiquities.
Once tried to add Lt. Commander Data to his collection.

Choose any player to immediately draw three new cards
from the top of their draw deck. Discard event after use.

Kivas Fajo - Collector

Although this diabolical, obsessed collector once drove Data to the point of disobeying his programming (Data discharged a Varon-T Disruptor at Kivas Fajo), he is an extremely helpful card in ST:TNG CCG. Played as an Event card, a chosen player may immediately draw three cards from his/her draw deck. Kivas Fajo – Collector is then discarded.

You might use this card early in the game to gain a strategic advantage by using it on yourself. Gaining three new cards early in the game is a definite strategic advantage (assuming you have built a good deck). Any time you have a greater number of cards in your hand to select, you will find that your options are increased greatly. Getting a ship and crew out sooner than your opponent can give you a major advantage, and the ability to draw three cards may give you that edge.

Later in the game, when the draw decks are dwindling down, you might use this card to force either you or your opponent to run out of cards. If you have a lead in points, you can gain victory by eliminating cards from the draw deck. The rules of ST:TNG CCG state that whoever is ahead in points when *either* player runs out of cards in a draw deck is declared the winner. Use this strategy with Kivas Fajo – Collector to gain victory in the late stages of a game.

EVENT

STAR TREK: THE NEXT GENERATION

Q-NET

Q used an enormous forcefield grid in space to stop the U.S.S. Enterprise in 2364.

Plays between two adjacent spaceline locations. No ship may pass the Q-Net unless 2 Diplomacy aboard.

T.M. ©, ℗ 1994 PARAMOUNT PICTURES.

Q-Net

Use Q-Net(s) to make movement of your opponent's ships difficult. The strategy is to play lots of Diplomacy in your deck, and then you can move effortlessly while your opponent may be stopped. Playing a Q-Net between a ship and its outpost can be frustrating to your opponent, and it will force him/her to have to get another ship out (with 2 Diplomacy onboard) to get the original ship back to the outpost.

As mentioned earlier, you can also use a Q-Net to stop an oncoming Borg Ship or an opponent's ship that's answering an Incoming Message (to return to the nearest outpost) or the call of the Cytherians. In any of these situations and many others, a Q-Net can be a very valuable card and should be considered a must in almost any deck. You might also consider adding Where No One Has Gone Before to your deck to make it even easier to get around Q-Nets.

EVENT

STAR TREK
THE NEXT GENERATION

TM, ®, © 1994 PARAMOUNT PICTURES.

RAISE THE STAKES

Weekly poker game aboard the *U.S.S. Enterprise*
honed the tactical and bluffing skills of many officers.

Your opponent must forfeit the game **OR** agree the
eventual winner may randomly select and keep one
card from loser's 60-card deck. (Cumulative.)

Raise the Stakes

This is a fun card with interesting tactical uses, although be forewarned that not everybody likes to play with it. Many players, especially collectors, do not like the idea potentially losing one of their cards, and thus many people have house rules against playing with it. This is because sometimes cards in their deck are quite valuable. Thus, if you are playing someone new for the first time, ask if they like playing with Raise the Stakes before using it.

For the more risk-taking, Kirk-like adventurous types, however, the Raise the Stakes card is unique. First, it takes some conceit to even stock it in your deck! You are taking up one card "slot" with a card that doesn't seem to further your aims. It seems like a card which has no offensive or defensive value!

Yet, it can be used to good effect, especially to bluff the opponent (similar to the way the doubling cube is used in backgammon). By playing the card, you inform your opponent that you are confident of victory, and lay down a challenge! The opponent must respond, and if you play it at just the right psychological moment (perhaps after the opponent has just suffered a setback, or when you appear to be set to attempt a high-point mission that might win the game for you), you can actually bluff the opponent into prematurely giving up the game! Give your best Will Riker poker face imitation as you play it! If the opponent accepts the challenge, he/she will still be placed under a psychological handicap by your move, and may alter his strategy at a time when he really shouldn't.

You may use it strategically to enjoy its effects at no risk to yourself. You do this by stocking some Kevin Uxbridge cards and keeping at least one in hand at all times. At the right time, play the Raise the Stakes. If the opponent continues the game and things turn sour for you, you will use Kevin Uxbridge to nullify the Raise the Stakes at the last moment!

EVENT

STAR TREK
THE NEXT GENERATION

RED ALERT

TM, ©, © 1994 PARAMOUNT PICTURES

RED ALERT!

The state of maximum crew and systems readiness aboard starships.

Plays on table. Allows you to play as many Ship, Personnel, and Equipment cards as desired each turn.

Red Alert!

The Red Alert allows you to rapidly deploy, in one turn, all Ship, Personnel, and Equipment cards in your hand. Normally these come out only at rate of one per turn. Thus, you can use it to flood the position relatively quickly with these important cards.

This rapid deployment possibility makes the card essential in the eyes of many players, especially during a long game when it may be used more than once in this manner. It is particularly effective if used in combination with an overall "quick-strike" strategy—either aiming to do missions quickly or to bring out attacking forces quickly. In such a strategy, you will be able to get more ships, personnel, and equipment into play than otherwise would be possible during the opening dozen or so moves of the game. Of course, if this is your strategy, you will need to stock several Red Alerts in your deck in order to insure one comes up early in the game (they don't do you much good at the bottom of the deck).

So many players think that Red Alert is an essential card that the designers have decided to come out with expansion cards that will mitigate it a little bit. The first of these will be the Yellow Alert card, which makes the Red Alert card less powerful (though still useful), in addition to having its own effects.

EVENT

STAR TREK
THE NEXT GENERATION

TM, ©, © 1994 PARAMOUNT PICTURES.

SUPERNOVA

The explosion of a star, usually caused by natural processes toward the end of its life cycle.

You must have Tox Uthat on table. Place atop any mission. Everything there is destroyed (discarded), but leave Mission card underneath for span reference.

Supernova

One of the most beautiful, and deadly, natural occuring phenomena in the universe is the explosion of a star—a supernova. You must have a Tox Uthat (Artifact) card in play before you can play the Supernova card. The power of the Supernova card is devastating, as you can choose any space/planet location and totally destroy *everything* (e.g. a planet, outpost, ship, personnel, Borg Ship, etc.) that's there. This powerful card can easily turn the tide in any game.

Try destroying your opponent's outpost with a Supernova to severely cripple him/her. Also, use a Supernova to destroy a Borg Ship (make sure it's on one of your opponent's missions) for an extra 45 points.

EVENT

STAR TREK
THE NEXT GENERATION

TM, ©, ℗ 1994 PARAMOUNT PICTURES

THE TRAVELER: TRANSCENDENCE

Benevolent humanoid from Tau Alpha C who could tran-
scend space and time with thought.

Place beside any player's draw deck. That player must
draw one extra card at the end of each turn. Also, while
in play, nullifies Static Warp Bubble. (Not cumulative.)

The Traveler: Transcendence

This mysterious, yet kind-hearted alien encountered the *U.S.S. Enterprise* on several occasions, ultimately becoming the mentor of Wesley Crusher, teaching him the secret of combining space, time, and thought. He thus has important positive powers in the game.

The main use of The Traveler is to play it on yourself, hopefully early in the game, allowing you an extra card draw at the end of each turn. Thus, at the investment of one card, you will earn extra power by more rapidly accumulating cards that you can use in play as the game progresses, providing you more choices. It is "not cumulative," so you can have only one in play at a time.

An extra card draw isn't always good, especially if you are behind in points and about to exhaust your deck. Thus, another way to effectively use The Traveler is to play it upon your opponent at such a time. It specifically says the player it is played upon "must" draw the extra card—there is no option. It will hasten the exhaustion of his/her deck, and thus potentially speed up your victory.

The Traveler also has the important ability to nullify any Static Warp Bubbles that were already played upon you or to prevent any new ones from being played upon you as long as it is in play.

Note that the name of this card "The Traveler: Transcendence" implies that there may be other card variations on The Traveler in the future!

⊚ **EVENT**

STAR TREK: THE NEXT GENERATION

TM ⊕ © 1994 PARAMOUNT PICTURES

WHERE NO ONE HAS GONE BEFORE

The Traveler transcends space with thought. Took the U.S.S. Enterprise to Galaxy M-33, then to an even greater extragalactic distance.

Plays on table. Allows all your ships to leave one end of the spaceline and enter the other end.

Where No One Has Gone Before

Just as The Traveler was able to move the *Enterprise* great distances using his thoughts, this Event card allows you to enter/exit either end of the spaceline and emerge at the opposite end. This ability can be useful for a number of reasons.

Most obviously, the ability to leave one end of the spaceline and enter at the opposite end really cuts down on the time it will take you to get to various missions. If you can get to those missions quicker than your opponent can get to his/her missions, then you stand a better chance of winning the game. If you have Where No One Has Gone Before in your deck, you can place your missions at the far ends of the spaceline hoping to get it into play and make completing those missions easier.

Another way to use this card is to play lots of Q-Nets and set up roadblocks for your opponent. Your opponent will be struggling to get from one mission to the other, while you can more easily do so by entering the spaceline from different ends.

Remember that Where No One Has Gone Before also affects the Borg Ship. This is a useful bit of information that can be used to your advantage to make your opponent's game difficult. You can wait until the Borg Ship Dilemma card is in play and moving along and then play Where No One Has Gone Before just as the ship is getting toward the end of the spaceline. Just be prepared to duck after you play this card with a Borg Ship in play!

INTERRUPT

THE NEXT GENERATION

TM, © & ℗ 1994 PARAMOUNT PICTURES.

AMANDA ROGERS

Female Q raised as a human on Earth. Was taken to the Q continuum by Q after she could not resist the benevolent use of her powers.

Nullifies any one Interrupt card just played (except Kevin Uxbridge or another Amanda Rogers) OR any one artifact just played as an Interrupt card.

Amanda Rogers

Amanda Rogers is a female Q, raised on Earth, who was unaware of her powers until encountering the *Enterprise*. She used her powers benevolently and was eventually taken into the Continuum by Q. This card can nullify any Interrupt card just played (except Kevin Uxbridge or another Amanda Rogers card) or any Artifact played as an Interrupt card. Playing as least two Amanda Rogers cards in any deck is probably a good idea.

This is a highly useful Interrupt card. Keep these in your hand to nullify any Interrupt cards your opponent might play. Use Res-Q or Palor Toff to bring back this card if your opponent plays lots of Interrupt cards.

Note that Amanda only works against an Interrupt card that was "just played." Thus, you must already have her in your hand if you want to play her—you could not, for example, use Palor Toff to regenerate her and then use her against an opponent's interrupt, because in that case the last interrupt "just played" was Palor Toff.

Also note that it is common courtesy when playing *any* Interrupt card to give the opponent a minimal amount of time to react to it, in case they want to Amanda Rogers it, before continuing play.

INTERRUPT

STAR TREK
THE NEXT GENERATION

TM ®, © 1994 PARAMOUNT PICTURES

CROSIS

Fanatical Borg lieutenant of Lore. Captured Lt. Commander Data with the lure of emotions.

Plays on Rogue Borg. Doubles their STRENGTH, including himself. Two Borg =4 STRENGTH each, three Borg =6 STRENGTH each, etc. (Not cumulative.)

Crosis

When Crosis is played with Rogue Borg Mercenaries he doubles everyone's Strength. For instance if you played 4 Rogue Borg Mercenaries and Crosis onto an opponent's ship, the Total Strength would be 50 (each Borg would be worth 5 since there are 5 of them counting Crosis, and then Crosis would double the total 5*5=25 doubled is 50). The effect of Crosis is not cumulative so, although you can play two Crosis cards, the Borg Strength is only doubled once.

Wait until you have Crosis and enough Rogue Borg Mercenaries in your hand to overpower a ship's crew, and then unleash Crosis and the mercenaries onto your opponent's ship all at once. You will defeat the ship's crew and leave Crosis onboard to stop any further attempts at manning the ship by your opponent. If you have the Lore Returns card, you can play it on the commandeered ship to allow you to take control of the ship and begin to attack other ships in your opponent's fleet.

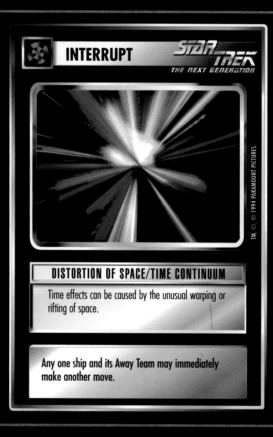

INTERRUPT

STAR TREK
THE NEXT GENERATION

TM, ©, ℗ 1994 PARAMOUNT PICTURES.

DISTORTION OF SPACE/TIME CONTINUUM

Time effects can be caused by the unusual warping or rifting of space.

Any one ship and its Away Team may immediately make another move.

Distortion of Space/Time Continuum

This Interrupt card allows any one ship and away team to immediately make another move, as if it had become "unstopped" after exhausting its normal movement that turn. Note that it applies only to a particular ship and its crew that you choose, and not to anything else.

The ability it gives you to get "double duty" out of a ship at the time of your choosing is very valuable, especially because there are a myriad of situations in which it can be useful. For example, you may be under attack by enemy ships and in need of some extra movement to reach safety that it can provide. Perhaps the game has reached a critical stage when getting the most out of every turn counts, and the ability to attempt and complete more than one mission during this turn could be crucial to the outcome. In such a case, using the card might allow you to get maximum efficiency at a key time.

It can also be used in battle situations (i.e., you move in and attack an opponent's ship with your Klingon cruiser, causing damage to the opponent). Normally the attacking ship and crew would be "stopped" by the battle, unable to do anything else this turn, and allowing the opponent the chance to try to escape next turn. But you play the Distortion card and move in for a second attack, this time destroying it! In such a situation you can also use the Distortion for "hit and run" tactics—for example, you move out and attack an opponent's ship and then play the Distortion to move back to safety before the opponent has a chance to bring in several ships to counter-attack you!

INTERRUPT

STAR TREK
THE NEXT GENERATION

TM ®, © 1994 PARAMOUNT PICTURES.

FULL PLANET SCAN

Sensor instruments can make detailed scans of a planet surface and atmosphere.

Glance at the Dilemma and Artifact cards located under one planet mission for twenty seconds.

Full Planet Scan

You probably know that before Picard would ever send an away team to a planet's surface he would order a scan of the planet's surface. Knowing that, it's probably a really good idea to follow in Jean-Luc's footsteps before sending your valuable crew down to meet the unknown.

The Full Planet Scan (Interrupt card) can be played before attempting any Planet Mission. It allows you to look at the dilemmas and artifacts under the mission card for twenty seconds. Twenty seconds (once you're very familiar with the various dilemmas in the ST:TNG CCG) should be ample time to determine the most effective Away Team for this mission.

Once you're equipped with an understanding of what (or who) awaits your Away Team on the surface of the planet, you can determine who (and how many) crew members to transport down. For example, if the first dilemma you see is a Female's Love Interest card, you might choose to avoid its effects completely by beaming down an all-male Away Team.

Knowing what's on the planet's surface will make your missions much easier, possibly save valuable crew from death, and frustrate your opponent. This makes the Full Planet Scan card a valuable one in any deck.

INTERRUPT

STAR TREK
THE NEXT GENERATION

TM, ® © 1994 PARAMOUNT PICTURES.

HUGH

The Federation named a rescued Borg, Hugh. When he returned, his newly acquired self-aware personality collapsed the Borg collective.

Nullifies attack by Borg Ship for this turn OR destroys (discard) all Rogue Borg at one location.

Hugh

This is a useful card to play in your deck since it nullifies any Borg attacks (either Borg Ship or Rogue Borg Mercenaries). Wait until you have a Hugh in your hand and then attempt the mission where you believe the Borg Ship is waiting. Or you can play a Borg Ship on one of your missions and unleash the Borg Ship safely if you have Hugh in your hand. You may also bring back Hugh with a Palor Toff or Res-Q card. (You can bet that Hugh will also figure prominently in expansion set cards which develop the Borg further!)

INTERRUPT

STAR TREK
THE NEXT GENERATION

TM, ® © 1994 PARAMOUNT PICTURES.

KEVIN UXBRIDGE

Immortal omnipotent being called a Douwd. Lived secretly as a human. Took a human wife who was killed by the Husnocks at Delta Rana IV.

Destroys any one Event card in play (except for Treaty cards) **OR** any one artifact in play as an Event card.

Kevin Uxbridge

Kevin Uxbridge is an extremely powerful being who once destroyed an entire race of beings with a single thought. He is the counterpart to Amanda Rogers, working against Event cards. Play this card to destroy any Event except treaties or any Artifact played as an Event.

Use at least two of these cards in your deck (if possible). The ability to nullify an Event card in play is powerful. Try to hold Kevin Uxbridge in your hand until your opponent plays a very powerful Event card. Use Res-Q or Palor Toff to bring back this card if your opponent plays lots of Event cards.

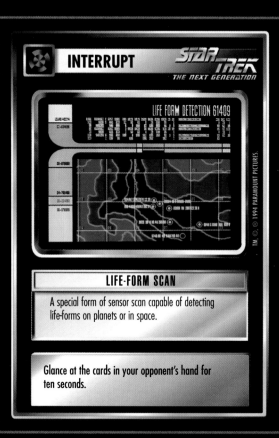

INTERRUPT

STAR TREK: THE NEXT GENERATION

LIFE FORM DETECTION 61409

TM, © ℗ 1994 PARAMOUNT PICTURES.

LIFE-FORM SCAN

A special form of sensor scan capable of detecting life-forms on planets or in space.

Glance at the cards in your opponent's hand for ten seconds.

Life-Form Scan

The Life-Form Scan Interrupt card allows you to look at your opponent's hand for ten seconds. This is certainly enough time to allow you the chance to know every card he/she holds and, more importantly, plan your strategy accordingly.

If you can determine that your opponent doesn't have a Kevin Uxbridge card (stops an Event card in play or any Artifact in play as an Event card) in hand, now might be the perfect time to play that critical Event card in your hand. Also, knowing your opponent has no one in hand with Engineer capability might make putting a Warp Core Breach card (destroys ship it's played on at the end of the opponent's next turn unless Engineer present by then) on a key ship a must.

Knowing the cards in your opponent's hand can really cripple his/her strategy and allow you to really play a key card at just the right moment. By combining the Life-Form Scan card with your overall strategy, you should be able to best pick when to play (and when not to) your important cards.

INTERRUPT

STAR TREK
THE NEXT GENERATION

TM, ®, © 1994 PARAMOUNT PICTURES.

PALOR TOFF — ALIEN TRADER

Rich merchant and trader from an unknown race. Friend of Kivas Fajo. Snappy dresser.

Exchange this card for any non-Personnel card in your discard pile.

Palor Toff – Alien Trader

This Interrupt card can be played to bring back to your hand any non-Personnel card in your discard pile. This can be very valuable to bring back any Event cards that your opponent has managed to get rid of and any Interrupts that you would like to replay.

An example of a devastating effect using Palor Toff – Alien Trader is to use the Betazoid Gift Box (which allows you to immediately search through your draw deck, find three cards, and place them in your hand) and then bring it back to your hand (using Palor Toff) and do it again! However, see discussions about further limitations on regenerating Artifacts on pages 81-82.

You might consider adding multiple Palor Toff – Alien Trader cards to your deck. The ability to bring back useful (and powerful) cards to your hand can really help gain you victory over any opponent.

TM. ©, ℗ 1994 PARAMOUNT PICTURES.

Q2

Member of the Q who observed Q's act of self-sacrifice and re-instated him in the Q continuum.

Nullifies any Amanda Rogers OR Kevin Uxbridge just played, OR nullifies any Q-related dilemma.

Q2

Another member of the Q Continuum. Although he was only ever referred to (by Q) as Q, he's called Q2 in the game. Play this card to nullify any Kevin Uxbridge, Amanda Rogers, or any Q-related dilemma. Since these cards can often affect the outcome of the game, being able to nullify them is a very valuable strategy.

You should try to keep a Q2 card in your hand until you're ready to play a key Event or Interrupt card (e.g. a Supernova, Hugh, Anti-Time Anomaly, or Genetronic Replicators). If your opponent tries to stop you (by playing a Kevin Uxbridge or Amanda Rogers), you can counter his/her move by playing a Q2 card.

INTERRUPT

STAR TREK: THE NEXT GENERATION

TM, ©, ® 1994 PARAMOUNT PICTURES.

ROGUE BORG MERCENARIES

Upon Hugh's return to the Borg collective, the Borg became self-aware. Soon, many unquestioningly followed their first leader, Lore.

Plays on any occupied ship. Battles crew now and at start of every players' turn. Two Borg =2 STRENGTH each, three =3 each, etc. Surviving Borg remain.

Rogue Borg
Mercenaries

The Borg and Rogue Borg elements of the game are features which will be developed further in expansion sets,
but are already an effective way to harass, damage, and
even control the opponent.

Rogue Borg have strength in numbers, and so when
planning to use them, a strategy that involves stocking
many of them in your deck is required to be effective.
The general strategy is to stock six or more in your
deck, and hold them in your hand as they come up until
you have a group of five or six you can unleash against
the opponent. They are played as an interrupt directly
onto his ship, where they attack the crew in a similar
manner to an away team battle until they are defeated
or they take over the ship. The more Rogue Borg you
stock, the sooner you will have a strong group to play.
If one of your Rogue Borg is Crosis, you can double
their attack strength.) Their total attack strength rises in
proportion to their number, being equal to the square of
their number. Two Rogue Borg are two Strength each =
4, three Rogue Borg are three each = 9, four are four
each = 16, etc.

A large group can thus devastate an opponent's crew,
although the battle may last many turns before the crew
is eliminated, and during that time the opponent might
bring up additional ships to beam over reinforcements!
These battles occur at the very beginning of each turn,
and of course as in all battles the personnel involved are
"stopped" for the remainder of the turn, which means
that they can have the additional effect of occupying the
opponent's forces, slowing their progress.

INTERRUPT

STAR TREK THE NEXT GENERATION

TM, ©, ℗ 1994 PARAMOUNT PICTURES.

SCAN

Sensor instruments can detect life signs and molecular signatures at a distance with accuracy.

Glance at the Dilemma and Artifact cards located under one space mission for twenty seconds.

Scan

When approaching an unfamiliar area of the galaxy, it's wise to scan for any unusual activity. You never know what you may encounter in space, and scanning the sector may enable you to not only complete your mission but also to get your ship and crew out safely.

The Scan card (played as an Interrupt) allows you to look under a Space Mission at the dilemma cards for twenty seconds. (Note: Although the Scan card states you can look at the dilemmas and artifacts found at the Space Mission, artifacts are currently only allowed to be seeded on Planet Missions.) After you know what awaits you at the Space Mission, you can determine whether you have the right personnel on board to overcome the Dilemma cards found there.

Because many of the Space Dilemmas can devastate (or destroy) your ship, it's imperative to know what you're facing before going blindly into the mission. (Although there will be times when you'll be without a Scan card and will have to do that anyway!) The key to strategy with the Scan card is to quickly see if there are any major catastrophes awaiting you (like Dilemmas that will destroy your ship unless certain personnel are aboard), and then make sure you can overcome those. If you find a Borg Ship, you'll know enough to leave quickly—at least until you have a way to deal with the Borg.

INTERRUPT

STAR TREK
THE NEXT GENERATION

TM, ®, © 1994 PARAMOUNT PICTURES

TEMPORAL RIFT

Time displacement caused by ultra high energy explosions such as that which affected the *U.S.S. Enterprise-C* at Narendra III.

Plays on any ship. Ship disappears and must reappear here after two of your full turns. Discard interrupt after reappearance.

Temporal Rift

Play this Interrupt card to cause any ship to disappear for two of your full turns. This can be a valuable way to either save your ships from attack or frustrate your opponent by making his/her ships disappear at key moments.

You can play a Temporal Rift on your opponent's ship just as he/she is attempting a mission and make your opponent wait two of your full turns before being able to reappear and reattempt the mission. You might also use the rift to save yourself from a Borg Ship that suddenly enters your sector. This card is useful to have because it can be used creatively by playing it on your ships, your opponent's ships, or Borg Ships.

INTERRUPT

STAR TREK: THE NEXT GENERATION

TM, ®, © 1994 PARAMOUNT PICTURES.

THE DEVIL

Ardra recreated the human mythical figure the Devil on Ventax II.

Destroys any one Treaty card on table **OR** one Horga'hn on table **OR** one Wind Dancer.

The Devil

Ardra created The Devil, among other illusions, during her attempt to take over Ventax II in the episode "Devil's Due." Fittingly, this card was given unusual uses of a symbolic nature which can be important—it nullifies three important cards.

First, it is currently the only way to destroy a Treaty card. (They are specifically immune to Kevin Uxbridge.) Use of The Devil in this way can at times be critical. Players who utilize multi-affiliation decks often count on their ability to create and maintain a Treaty, in order for their cards to have the coordination that they need to be effective in play otherwise, their forces are divided). If you believe your opponent will be using Treaties, surprising him with The Devil will often be very unpleasant!

It also has other uses, including destroying the very strong Horga'hn card (which also is not vulnerable to Kevin Uxbridge). As discussed earlier, acquiring this artifact and getting it into play is a powerful move, often the result of a concerted strategy by the opponent. Destroying it with The Devil can frustrate the opponent's plans and make his attempt to acquire the Horga'hn a waste of time!

Finally, The Devil also can be played to surpass the tough Wind Dancer dilemma card, which otherwise is often a real stopper, especially for Romulans.

The limitations of the three specific uses of The Devil can be a drawback—if you never encounter any of these three cards The Devil currently has no other use. But the ones it does affect can be critical, and it has flexible uses within that group.

INTERRUPT

STAR TREK
THE NEXT GENERATION

TM, ®, © 1994 PARAMOUNT PICTURES

VULCAN MINDMELD

Ancient Vulcan ritual which telepathically links minds to intimately share each other's thoughts and knowledge.

Allows all Mindmeld personnel, at one location, to add to their skills. For one turn, add all of the skills of another personnel who is present.

Vulcan Mindmeld

As long as there have been Vulcans there has been the Mindmeld. This technique allows a Vulcan to gain, from the person whose mind they join, all the knowledge and thoughts of the person. In the game, you can use this technique to complete missions and overcome dilemmas by gaining all the abilities of another member of the crew.

You have Sarek on the *Enterprise* as you approach an unknown area of space. A strange infection invades the ship (Tsiolkovsky's Infection) and Beverly Crusher is overwhelmed in the sick bay trying to figure out a cure for the disease. Sarek might mindmeld with Beverly (by playing the Vulcan Mindmeld card) and gain her Medical ability. Now Sarek can help Beverly overcome the dilemma (Beverly has Medical x 2 and Sarek mind-melds to gain Medical) as they have 3 Medical (the Tsiolkovsky Infection dilemma requires 3 Medical to overcome) between them, and the *Enterprise* can proceed with the mission.

The Vulcan Mindmeld might also be used to complete those missions that require multiple skills (e.g. Astrophysics x 2). You can have a Vulcan Mindmeld with someone who has Astrophysics and now possibly complete the mission. Thus, the flexibility of possible uses for the card makes it potentially more valuable than Equipment cards. Also, note that *all* Vulcans with mindmeld skill at the same location are affected by the card.

There may be other cards which use mindmeld skills in the future.

INTERRUPT

STAR TREK: THE NEXT GENERATION

TM, © ℗ 1994 PARAMOUNT PICTURES.

WORMHOLE

An unstable tunnel through subspace that links to locations in normal space/time.

Requires two wormholes. Play one on any ship just as it begins to move. Play the other where the ship immediately emerges. Discard wormholes.

Wormhole

The Wormhole anomaly is one that has plagued the *Enterprise* (and many other ships) on many episodes. The unpredictability of the wormhole can (and has) wreaked havoc more than once in the series, and it can do much the same thing in the card game. You need to play two Wormhole cards, both played as an Interrupt, in order to use this card. The first card is played on the ship that you want to put into the wormhole, and the second is placed anywhere on the spaceline as where the ship will reappear.

You could wormhole an opponent's ship to the far side of the spaceline just when your opponent is approaching a mission that he/she can complete. You might wormhole a ship right into the path of an oncoming Borg Ship (very nasty). Perhaps you might use the Wormhole cards to send a ship answering a Cytherians call back to the far end of the spaceline. Another strategy would be to use the cards to place a ship without 2 Diplomacy on the other side of a Q-Net (which requires 2 Diplomacy to pass).

Don't forget that you can also use the Wormhole cards on your own ships and on the Borg Ship. This can mean that you can move your ship from one end of the spaceline to the other, and that might mean winning the game if the mission you need to complete is there. You can also use the cards to save yourself from Borg by sending either your ship or the Borg Ship to another part of the galaxy.

❖ *Husnock Ship*

TM ® © 1994 PARAMOUNT PICTURES

UNKNOWN CLASS

With a single thought, Kevin Uxbridge killed the entire Husnock race (50 billion lives) everywhere in the universe. Their powerful ships remain.

 Holodeck, Tractor Beam

| RANGE 6 | WEAPONS 9 | SHIELDS 12 |

Husnock Ship

This ship is valuable because it has Shields of 12. It can be a great defensive ship to bring along with your other ships. Since it is a Non-Aligned ship, it can be used by any of the affiliations. It is the only ship that can, without additional boosts to its shields, survive a direct attack by the Borg Ship.

U.S.S. Enterprise

STAR TREK
THE NEXT GENERATION

TM, ®, © 1994 PARAMOUNT PICTURES

GALAXY CLASS

The fifth Starfleet ship named *Enterprise*, launched in 2363. Built at the Utopia Planetia shipyards orbiting Mars.

Holodeck, Tractor Beam

| RANGE | 9 | WEAPONS | 8 | SHIELDS | 9 |

USS Enterprise

The most powerful ship in the Federation fleet—its range, shields, and weapons make it a threat whenever you (or your opponent) gets it into play. A good strategy when playing the *Enterprise* is to use missions with high spans (the number at the bottom of the Mission card which indicates how large an area of space this mission takes up). This way your ship will be able to travel the spaceline more easily than your opponent's ships.

Since the *Enterprise* is equipped with a Holodeck, you may want to add holographic personnel to your deck and play a lot of Space Missions. Finding Space Missions that require Physics, Astrophysics, or Engineer will allow you to play Sir Isaac Newton, Albert Einstein, and Dr. Leah Brahms.

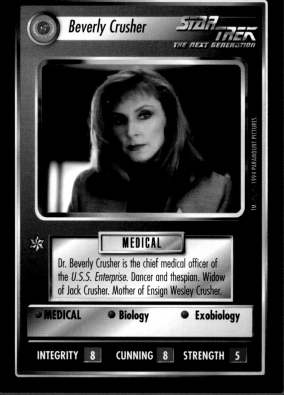

Beverly Crusher

STAR TREK
THE NEXT GENERATION

TM ® © 1994 PARAMOUNT PICTURES

MEDICAL

Dr. Beverly Crusher is the chief medical officer of the *U.S.S. Enterprise.* Dancer and thespian. Widow of Jack Crusher. Mother of Ensign Wesley Crusher.

● **MEDICAL**   ● **Biology**   ● **Exobiology**

INTEGRITY `8`   CUNNING `8`   STRENGTH `5`

Beverly Crusher

Chief Medical Officer aboard the Federation's flagship. She has Medical x2, Biology, and Exobiology skills and has command ability. Her Integrity and Cunning of 8 each make her one of the higher rated Federation personnel in those areas.

She has only 3 abilities, but she is Medical x2, which alone can be enough to use with a Genetronic Replicators (Event) card to prevent any of your Away Team members from being killed. She can also single handedly complete a mission (Evaluate Terraforming).

STAR TREK
THE NEXT GENERATION

Data

TM, ®, © 1994 PARAMOUNT PICTURES.

OFFICER

Lt. Commander Data is a sentient android created by Dr. Noonien Soong. Has positronic brain. Desires to be human. Once left his head in San Francisco.

- ENGINEER
- Computer Skill x2
- Music
- Astrophysics
- Exobiology

| INTEGRITY | 8 | CUNNING | 12 | STRENGTH | 12 |

Data

Data is the only android in Starfleet. Although he is an android, he has exhibited a better understand of humanity than have some humans. He was judged a sentient being by an official court (Jean-Luc Picard represented Lieutenant Commander Data at the hearing).

Arguably the most powerful Personnel card in the game, his Cunning and Strength of 12 make him an excellent choice for almost any Planet Mission. His engineering, astrophysics, and superior computer skill also make him an extremely effective card to play. Finally, he can complete a mission by himself (Investigate Time Continuum).

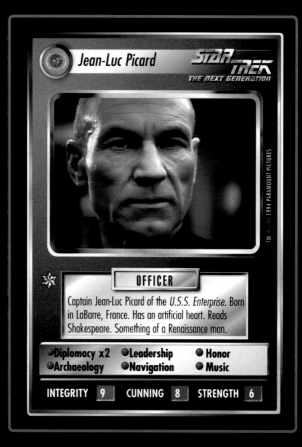

Jean-Luc Picard

OFFICER

Captain Jean-Luc Picard of the *U.S.S. Enterprise*. Born in LaBarre, France. Has an artificial heart. Reads Shakespeare. Something of a Renaissance man.

- Diplomacy x2
- Archaeology
- Leadership
- Navigation
- Honor
- Music

INTEGRITY	9	CUNNING	8	STRENGTH	6

TM, ® & © 1994 PARAMOUNT PICTURES

Jean-Luc Picard

Captain Jean-Luc Picard commands the most powerful ship in the Federation—the *U.S.S. Enterprise*. His strong command is invaluable on the Bridge, although he has on occasion commanded an Away Team (even though Commander Riker always objects). A man of high integrity (Integrity =9), he is respected by every member of his crew. He was once assimilated into the Borg consciousness and became Locutus (perhaps an expansion card?) of Borg. That experience has deeply affected Picard, and the Borg are never far from his thoughts. (Note: The image on the Jean-Luc Picard card is the moment the Enterprise and Picard first encounter the Borg.)

Picard is the only person in the game with six abilities (Honor, Music, Archaeology, Navigation, Diplomacy x2, and Leadership) so he can be very strategically important in a Federation deck. One strategy with Picard is to play a lot of Q-Nets (which require 2 Diplomacy to pass) on the spaceline. You should be able to pass while your opponent may have difficulty.

Roga Danar

STAR TREK
THE NEXT GENERATION

TM, © 1994 PARAMOUNT PICTURES.

SECURITY

Angosian male. Biochemically altered into a formidable perfect warrior ranked *Subhadar*.

● ENGINEER ● Computer Skill ● Biology
● Leadership

| INTEGRITY | 5 | CUNNING | 9 | STRENGTH | 12 |

Roga Danar

Perhaps the most formidable human opponent the *U.S.S. Enterprise* ever encountered, Roga Danar is a biochemically created perfect soldier from Angosia who succeeded in outwitting Lieutenant Commander Data and outfighting Lieutenant Worf to achieve his goals.

He is one of the strongest Personnel cards, with 9 Cunning and 12 Strength. He also possesses many skills, including both Security and Engineer, plus the ability to command ships. This makes him an excellent all-around personnel on any crew or Away Team.

Most importantly, he is a non-aligned character and thus can be used in any deck. As such he is almost always a good choice for one of the personnel in you deck, capable of working with any affiliation strategy.

Sarek

STAR TREK THE NEXT GENERATION

TM & © 1994 PARAMOUNT PICTURES

V.I.P.

Illustrious Vulcan Federation ambassador. Over 200 years old. Married at least three times: to a Vulcan princess, to Amanda and to Perrin. Father of Spock.

● Diplomacy x3 ● Mindmeld

INTEGRITY **9** CUNNING **10** STRENGTH **3**

Sarek

Sarek, besides being the father to Spock, was a formidable diplomat—regal, logical, and intensely persuasive. Vulcan Federation Ambassador, he is credited with negotiating many historic treaties in his 200+ years of life.

His Personnel card in ST:TNG CCG reflects this in being the only Personnel with Diplomacy x3, which is often useful for key missions or dilemmas that require lots of diplomacy. (Use Sarek to pass Q-Nets with ease, for example.)

His mindmeld skill can also be valuable as a source to gain additional skills, and gives him further flexibility when combined with Vulcan Mindmeld cards (or other future cards that utilize Mindmeld skill). He also has exceptionally high Cunning (10).

The Data Laughing card is a special card available only through the purchase of this strategy guide. The card's image is taken from the "Deja Q" episode of *Star Trek: The Next Generation* in which the entity Q loses his powers and becomes mortal. One of Q's enemies, the Calamarain, seek out the now defenseless Q and almost succeed in killing him. Data's heroic actions save Q, and Q bestows upon Data a moment of laughter as a reward for his unselfishness.

This image of Data from "Deja Q" was chosen not just because of Data's popularity, but also because this experience was a high point for the Data character. Data Laughing features a very significant moment in the ST:TNG series because Data always showed curiosity about humor. His quest to become more human by learning more about human qualities is never ending, but with the gift of laughter Data knows—if only for a moment—one human emotion.

Data Laughing

The Data Laughing card is a very powerful card in the ST:TNG CCG—not only in the original set, but also in the Alternate Universe and Q Continuum expansion sets (to be released later this year). Data Laughing is an Interrupt card which nullifies Calamarain (which promises to be a nasty card in the Q Continuum expansion set) OR doubles Data's Head (which will have a powerful effect in the Alternate Universe expansion set) OR retakes one ship controlled by Lore Returns (so Lore and Rogue Borg now follow your direction).

Lore Returns, in combination with Rogue Borg cards, has proven to be a strategically important card in the game. A player who uses Rogue Borg to eliminate a ship's crew can then use Lore Returns to command that ship and attack other ships (or beam down an Away Team of Rogue Borg to battle on a planet's surface). Playing the Data Laughing Interrupt card, a player can now retake the ship and control Lore and the Rogue Borg.

The staff at Decipher made this card not only very collectible, but also very valuable for game play. The card's picture has all the quality and clarity of the other cards in the set, the usefulness is very high (and will grow when the expansion sets are released), and the card will only be available through the purchase of this strategy guide— which will increase its value for collectors. We are proud to offer the Data Laughing card FREE through this exclusive mail-in offer.

Card Checklist

Freq.	Type	Card	Affiliation
R	Artifact	Betazoid Gift Box	
R	Artifact	Horga'hn	
R	Artifact	Interphase Generator	
R	Artifact	Kurlan Naiskos	
R	Artifact	Thought Maker	
R	Artifact	Time Travel Pod	
R	Artifact	Tox Uthat	
R	Artifact	Varon-T Disruptor	
R	Artifact	Vulcan Stone Of Gol	
U	Dilemma	Alien Abduction	
U	Dilemma	Alien Parasites	
C	Dilemma	Anaphasic Organism	
R	Dilemma	Ancient Computer	
C	Dilemma	Archer	
R	Dilemma	Armus — Skin of Evil	
R	Dilemma	Barclay's Protomorphosis Disease	
U	Dilemma	Birth Of "Junior"	
R	Dilemma	Borg Ship	
U	Dilemma	Chalnoth	
U	Dilemma	Cosmic String Fragment	
R	Dilemma	Crystalline Entity	
R	Dilemma	Cytherians	

Freq.	Type	Card	Affiliation
U	Dilemma	El-Adrel Creature	
C	Dilemma	Female's Love Interest	
U	Dilemma	Firestorm	
U	Dilemma	Gravitic Mine	
U	Dilemma	Hologram Ruse	
U	Dilemma	Hyper-Aging	
C	Dilemma	Iconian Computer Weapon	
C	Dilemma	Impassable Door	
C	Dilemma	Male's Love Interest	
U	Dilemma	Matriarchal Society	
C	Dilemma	Menthar Booby Trap	
C	Dilemma	Microbiotic Colony	
C	Dilemma	Microvirus	
R	Dilemma	Ktarian Game	
R	Dilemma	Nagilum	
U	Dilemma	Nanites	
U	Dilemma	Nausicaans	
U	Dilemma	Nitrium Metal Parasites	
U	Dilemma	Null Space	
C	Dilemma	Phased Matter	
U	Dilemma	Portal Guard	
R	Dilemma	Q	
U	Dilemma	Radioactive Garbage Scow	
U	Dilemma	Rebel Encounter	
U	Dilemma	Rem Fatigue Hallucinations	
R	Dilemma	Sarjenka	
U	Dilemma	Shaka, When The Walls Fell	
U	Dilemma	Tarellian Plague Ship	
R	Dilemma	Temporal Causality Loop	
R	Dilemma	Tsiolkovsky Infection	
U	Dilemma	Two-Dimensional Creatures	
R	Dilemma	Wind Dancer	
C	Equipment	Engineering Kit	
C	Equipment	Engineering Padd	
C	Equipment	Federation Padd	
C	Equipment	Klingon Disruptor	
C	Equipment	Klingon Padd	
C	Equipment	Medical Kit	

Freq.	Type	Card	Affiliation
C	Equipment	Medical Tricorder	
C	Equipment	ROM Disruptor	
C	Equipment	ROM Padd	
C	Equipment	Starfleet Type II Phaser	
C	Equipment	Tricorder	
U	Event	Alien Probe	
R	Event	Anti-Time Anomaly	
C	Event	Atmospheric Ionization	
R	Event	Bynars Weapon Enhancement	
U	Event	Distortion Field	
C	Event	Espionage: FED On KLG	
C	Event	Espionage: KLG On FED	
C	Event	Espionage: ROM On FED	
C	Event	Espionage: ROM On KLG	
U	Event	Gaps In Normal Space	
U	Event	Genetronic Replicator	
R	Event	Goddess of Empathy	
U	Event	Holo-Projectors	
U	Event	Kivas Fajo — Collector	
R	Event	Lore Returns	
R	Event	Lore's Fingernail	
U	Event	Masaka Transformations	
U	Event	Metaphasic Shields	
U	Event	Neural Servo Device	
U	Event	Nutational Shields	
C	Event	Pattern Enhancers	
C	Event	Plasma Fire	
C	Event	Q-Net	
U	Event	Raise The Stakes	
C	Event	Red Alert!	
C	Event	Res-Q	
C	Event	Spacedock	
C	Event	Static Warp Bubble	
C	Event	Subspace Warp Rift	
R	Event	Supernova	
U	Event	Telepathic Alien Kidnappers	
C	Event	Tetryon Field	
U	Event	The Traveler: Transcendence	

Freq.	Type	Card	Affiliation
C	Event	Treaty: FED/KLG	
C	Event	Treaty: FED/ROM	
C	Event	Treaty: ROM/KLG	
R	Event	Warp Core Breach	
C	Event	Where No One Has Gone Before	
R	Interrupt	Alien Groupie	
U	Interrupt	Amanda Rogers	
C	Interrupt	Asteroid Sanctuary	
U	Interrupt	Auto-Destruct Sequence	
R	Interrupt	Crosis	
C	Interrupt	Disruptor Overload	
U	Interrupt	Distortion Of Space/Time Continuum	
U	Interrupt	Energy Vortex	
C	Interrupt	Emergency Transporter Armbands	
C	Interrupt	Escape Pod	
U	Interrupt	Full Planet Scan	
R	Interrupt	Honor Challenge	
R	Interrupt	Hugh	
U	Interrupt	Incoming Message — FED	
U	Interrupt	Incoming Message — KLG	
U	Interrupt	Incoming Message — ROM	
R	Interrupt	Jaglom Shrek — Information Broker	
U	Interrupt	Kevin Uxbridge	
R	Interrupt	Klingon Death Yell	
C	Interrupt	Klingon Right Of Vengeance	
U	Interrupt	Life-Form Scan	
C	Interrupt	Long-Range Scan	
C	Interrupt	Loss Of Orbital Stability	
U	Interrupt	Near-Warp Transport	
C	Interrupt	Palor Toff — Alien Trader	
C	Interrupt	Particle Fountain	
U	Interrupt	Q2	
C	Interrupt	Rogue Borg Mercenaries	
C	Interrupt	Scan	
C	Interrupt	Ship Seizure	
C	Interrupt	Subspace Interference	
U	Interrupt	Subspace Schism	
C	Interrupt	Tachyon Detection Grid	

Freq.	Type	Card	Affiliation
U	Interrupt	Temporal Rift	
R	Interrupt	The Devil	
U	Interrupt	The Juggler	
U	Interrupt	Transwarp Conduit	
U	Interrupt	Vulcan Mindmeld	
C	Interrupt	Wormhole	
R	Mission	Avert Disaster	
U	Mission	Cloaked Mission	
C	Mission	Covert Installation	
U	Mission	Covert Rescue	
R	Mission	Cultural Observation	
U	Mission	Diplomacy Mission	
R	Mission	Evaluate Terraforming	
C	Mission	Excavation	
U	Mission	Evacuation	
R	Mission	Explore Black Cluster	
R	Mission	Explore Dyson Sphere	
R	Mission	Explore Typhone Expanse	
U	Mission	Expose Covert Supply	
R	Mission	Extraction	
C	Mission	Fever Emergency	
U	Mission	First Contact	
R	Mission	Hunt for DNA Program	
R	Mission	Iconia Investigation	
R	Mission	Investigate "Shattered Space"	
R	Mission	Investigate Alien Probe	
C	Mission	Investigate Anomaly	
R	Mission	Investigate Disappearance	
R	Mission	Investigate Disturbance	
R	Mission	Investigate Massacre	
R	Mission	Investigate Raid	
R	Mission	Investigate Rogue Comet	
R	Mission	Investigate Sighting	
R	Mission	Investigate Time Continuum	
R	Mission	Khitomer Research	
U	Mission	Krios Suppression	
R	Mission	Medical Relief	
R	Mission	New Contact	

Freq.	Type	Card	Affiliation
R	Mission	Pegasus Search	
U	Mission	Plunder Site	
C	Mission	Relief Mission	
C	Mission	Repair Mission	
U	Mission	Restore Errant Moon	
R	Mission	Sarthong Plunder	
U	Mission	Secret Salvage	
R	Mission	Seek Life-form	
U	Mission	Strategic Diversion	
R	Mission	Study "Hole In Space"	
R	Mission	Study Lonka Pulsar	
R	Mission	Study Nebula	
C	Mission	Study Plasma Streamer	
C	Mission	Study Stellar Collision	
R	Mission	Survey Mission	
C	Mission	Test Mission	
R	Mission	Wormhole Negotiations	
C	Outpost	Federation	
C	Outpost	Klingon	
C	Outpost	Romulan	
R	Personnel	Albert Einstein	FED
R	Personnel	Alidar Jarok	ROM
R	Personnel	Alynna Nechayev	FED
U	Personnel	Alexander Rozhenko	FED
U	Personnel	Alyssa Ogawa	FED
U	Personnel	Amarie	NON
R	Personnel	B'Etor	KLG
C	Personnel	B'iJik	KLG
C	Personnel	Batrell	KLG
U	Personnel	Ba'el	KLG
U	Personnel	Baran	NON
U	Personnel	Benjamin Maxwell	FED
R	Personnel	Beverly Crusher	FED
U	Personnel	Bochra	ROM
U	Personnel	Bok	NON
C	Personnel	Calloway	FED
C	Personnel	Christopher Hobson	FED
C	Personnel	Darian Wallace	FED

Freq.	Type	Card	Affiliation
R	Personnel	Data	FED
R	Personnel	Deanna Troi	FED
U	Personnel	Devinoni Ral	NON
C	Personnel	Divok	KLG
C	Personnel	Dr. Farek	NON
R	Personnel	Dr. La Forge	FED
R	Personnel	Dr. Leah Brahms	FED
U	Personnel	Dr. Reyga	NON
U	Personnel	Dr. Selar	FED
C	Personnel	Dukath	KLG
R	Personnel	Duras	KLG
U	Personnel	Etana Jol	NON
U	Personnel	Eric Pressman	FED
U	Personnel	Evek	NON
U	Personnel	Exocomp	FED
U	Personnel	Fek'lhr	KLG
U	Personnel	Fleet Admiral Shanthi	FED
C	Personnel	Galathon	ROM
C	Personnel	Giusti	FED
R	Personnel	Geordi La Forge	FED
C	Personnel	Gorath	KLG
C	Personnel	Gorta	NON
R	Personnel	Gowron	KLG
U	Personnel	Hannah Bates	FED
U	Personnel	Ishara Yar	NON
C	Personnel	J'Ddan	KLG
C	Personnel	Jaron	ROM
R	Personnel	Jean-Luc Picard	FED
U	Personnel	Jenna D'Sora	FED
C	Personnel	Jera	ROM
U	Personnel	Jo'Bril	NON
R	Personnel	K'Ehleyr	FED
U	Personnel	K'mpec	KLG
U	Personnel	K'Tal	KLG
C	Personnel	K'Tesh	KLG
U	Personnel	K'Vada	KLG
R	Personnel	Kahless	KLG
U	Personnel	Kareel Odan	FED

Freq.	Type	Card	Affiliation
R	Personnel	Kargan	KLG
U	Personnel	Kell	KLG
C	Personnel	Klag	KLG
C	Personnel	Kle'eg	KLG
U	Personnel	Konmel	KLG
U	Personnel	Koral	KLG
U	Personnel	Koroth	KLG
U	Personnel	Korris	KLG
C	Personnel	Kromm	KLG
R	Personnel	Kurak	KLG
R	Personnel	Kurn	KLG
U	Personnel	L'Kor	KLG
R	Personnel	Lursa	KLG
R	Personnel	Lwaxana Troi	FED
C	Personnel	Linda Larson	FED
C	Personnel	McKnight	FED
R	Personnel	Mendak	ROM
C	Personnel	Mendon	FED
U	Personnel	Morag	KLG
R	Personnel	Morgan Bateson	FED
U	Personnel	Mot the Barber	FED
U	Personnel	Mirok	ROM
U	Personnel	Movar	ROM
U	Personnel	N'Vek	ROM
C	Personnel	Narik	NON
R	Personnel	Neela Daren	FED
U	Personnel	Neral	ROM
U	Personnel	Nikolai Rozhenko	FED
U	Personnel	Norah Satie	FED
U	Personnel	Nu'Daq	KLG
U	Personnel	Ocett	NON
C	Personnel	Palteth	ROM
U	Personnel	Pardek	ROM
U	Personnel	Parem	ROM
R	Personnel	Reginald Barclay	FED
R	Personnel	Richard Galen	FED
U	Personnel	Riva	FED
R	Personnel	Ro Laren	FED

Freq.	Type	Card	Affiliation
R	Personnel	Roga Danar	NON
R	Personnel	Sarek	FED
R	Personnel	Satelk	FED
R	Personnel	Sela	ROM
C	Personnel	Selok	ROM
R	Personnel	Shelby	FED
C	Personnel	Simon Tarses	FED
R	Personnel	Sir Isaac Newton	FED
U	Personnel	Sirna Kolrami	FED
C	Personnel	Sito Jaxa	FED
U	Personnel	Soren	FED
U	Personnel	T'Pan	FED
U	Personnel	Taibak	ROM
C	Personnel	Taitt	FED
C	Personnel	Takket	ROM
C	Personnel	Tallus	ROM
R	Personnel	Tam Elbrun	FED
C	Personnel	Tarus	ROM
R	Personnel	Tasha Yar	FED
C	Personnel	Taul	ROM
C	Personnel	Taurik	FED
U	Personnel	Tebok	ROM
C	Personnel	Thei	ROM
R	Personnel	Thomas Riker	FED
U	Personnel	Toby Russell	FED
U	Personnel	Tokath	ROM
R	Personnel	Tomalak	ROM
C	Personnel	Tomek	ROM
U	Personnel	Toq	KLG
U	Personnel	Torak	KLG
U	Personnel	Toral	KLG
R	Personnel	Toreth	ROM
C	Personnel	Torin	KLG
U	Personnel	Vagh	KLG
C	Personnel	Varel	ROM
R	Personnel	Vash	FED
C	Personnel	Vekma	KLG
C	Personnel	Vekor	NON
R	Personnel	Wesley Crusher	FED

Freq.	Type	Card	Affiliation
R	Personnel	William T. Riker	FED
R	Personnel	Worf	FED
C	Ship	Combat Vessel	NON
C	Ship	D'deridex	ROM
R	Ship	Devoras	ROM
R	Ship	Haakona	ROM
U	Ship	Husnock Ship	NON
R	Ship	IKC Bortas	KLG
R	Ship	IKC Buruk	KLG
C	Ship	IKC K'Vort	KLG
R	Ship	IKC Hegh'ta	KLG
R	Ship	IKC Pagh	KLG
R	Ship	IKC Qu'Vat	KLG
C	Ship	IKC Vor'Cha	KLG
U	Ship	IKC Vorn	KLG
R	Ship	Khazara	ROM
C	Ship	Mercenary Ship	NON
R	Ship	Pi	ROM
C	Ship	Runabout	FED
C	Ship	Science Vessel	ROM
C	Ship	Scout Vessel	ROM
C	Ship	Type VI Shuttlecraft	FED
R	Ship	USS Brittain	FED
R	Ship	USS Enterprise	FED
C	Ship	USS Excelsior	FED
C	Ship	USS Galaxy	FED
R	Ship	USS Hood	FED
C	Ship	USS Miranda	FED
C	Ship	USS Nebula	FED
C	Ship	USS Oberth	FED
R	Ship	USS Phoenix	FED
U	Ship	USS Sutherland	FED
R	Ship	USS Yamato	FED
C	Ship	Yridian Shuttle	NON
C	Ship	Zibalian Transport	NON

Answers to Your Questions About Game Play

This game has a very deep basic structure. Each card tells you what it does, but the combinations of cards in play are incalculable. As mentioned at the beginning of the rules, if an unexpected twist comes up that isn't in the rulebook, use common *Star Trek* sense to resolve it. There are, however, a number of twists that players inquire about more often than others. This Q&A discusses some of the most common rules and questions (alphabetically by topic). Although this list is by no means exhaustive, it should prove quite useful when struggling to interpret certain ambiguities in the game. Remember, you can always make a house rule or contact Decipher's game information services (see Appendix 4) to resolve seemingly unresolvable situations.

The following is a list of the topics covered. If you can't find what you're looking for, try cross-referencing it with another topic discussed in the question. For instance, "Can Rogue Borg attack a cloaked ship?" appears under "Cloaked Ships," not "Borg."

Alliances and Outposts

Q: Can you create an alliance during the game if you don't have outposts representing both affiliations in play?

A: Yes. (1) If you start out with two outposts but one of them gets destroyed, you can still create the treaty. While the treaty is in effect, all the new personnel can come in at the remaining outpost.

(2) If you start with only one outpost from the beginning, you can also still create an alliance, although you can only bring in the mixed-affiliation personnel at the outpost after you establish the treaty.

Q: If you attempt a mission from an outpost, with no ships involved, and you encounter a dilemma targeting a ship, do you ignore it and go on?

A: If the dilemma specifically affects the ship only, then it has no effect since there is no ship. However, if the dilemma affects the crew, it does have an effect. For example, The Tarellian Plague Ship says, "All ship's crew immediately die from plague unless Medical volunteers to permanently beam over (discarded) to Tarellians...." This applies to the crew from the outpost as well —you would have to beam over a Medical Personnel or your whole crew is toast.

Q: Are there non-aligned outposts?

A: Not in the initial 363 cards, but there will be a Neutral Outpost in the expansion sets, and possibly others.

Attacking

Q: Can the Federation attack Romulans or Klingons on planets?

A: Not normally, no. The prohibition against the Federation *initiating* attacks extends to Away Team battles, too, although you might see special cards in the future that do allow it under certain circumstances.

Q: If you are playing, for example, Federation and Klingons without a treaty, can your Federation ships/personnel get "dragged into" a battle if your Klingons are attacked, or does the Federation only get to counterattack when they are *directly* attacked? What is the situation if a treaty *is* in effect?

A: With no treaty in effect, the Federation could *not* attack, with a treaty they could.

Q: The Federation cannot initiate attacks, but are allowed to retaliate. Does this include a second Federation ship that I'd like to bring to the aid of another that is under attack?

A: Once a battle gets started (Away Team or Ship battles), the battle lasts for as long as the players choose to continue it on successive turns, until the ship(s) are destroyed or until one player breaks off the battle in some fashion. If your ship attacks the opponent and both ships are damaged, your opponent can either break off the battle or continue it by counter-attacking you on his/her turn. The counter-attack we consider to be continuing the same "battle" that you started, rather than a separate battle. In this case it is possible to bring in new ships to join the battle. If a Federation ship is attacked in this way, not only can it counter-attack, but you can "call in" nearby Federation ships to come to your aid in the battle.

Q: Federation forces are normally not supposed to initiate an attack. Does this include a situation in which there are Klingons aboard a Federation ship under a treaty?

A: If you are playing an alliance under treaty of Federation/Klingon, then situations may arise in which you have Klingons aboard a Federation ship. It is possible for a ship with a mixed crew like this to initiate an attack—but *only* if a Klingon aboard has Leadership skill (otherwise, no one would obey him and the Federation rules against attack would prevail). The same would apply with Federation/Romulan treaties and mixed crews.

Artifacts

Q: Kurlan Naiskos triples a ship's stats if all seven personnel types are on board. Would an Officer who also has Medical skills, for example, count as both for this purpose?

A: Yes—it doesn't say Classifications, it says Types.

Artificial Lifeforms

Q: Are the artificial personnel like Data and Exocomps affected by cards like Dilemmas or Events that normally would only affect "natural beings?"

A: As a general rule, Androids and Exocomps, etc., would not be affected by cards that specifically affect living things—as long as there is good reason to believe they logically would not be. For example, the Hyper-Aging card would not affect beings

which do not age at all. Usually comm
sense will answer any particular instar
this type.

Q: Are non-sleepers like Data affe
by the REM Sleep card?

A: The point about the REM Sleep
lem is that it drives the crew c
until they destroy the ship. Even thous
some of the crew might be non-sleepe
Exocomps, and thus not personally aff
they will still be destroyed when the r
the crew goes crazy, and thus are affe
by the card. However, you might use a
"house rule" for this rare exception: I
majority of the crew are non-sleepers,
the REM Sleep dilemma has no effect
because not enough of the crew goes

Away Teams

Q: When all Away Teams are stop
can a new Away Team be form
beamed down to continue?

A: Yes, as long as it is made up of Personnel who aren't already "stopped" for that turn. For example, if your initial Away Team hits a Sarjenka Dilemma and is stopped, you might bring up another ship, beam down another Away Team, and try the mission with them. Of course, the personnel in the initial Away Team can't participate because they are stopped.

Q: If you beam an Away Team to a mission from two separate ships, do they come together as one Away Team?

A: Yes—if you beam them both down it is assumed they are intended to be there together. If you want to operate them separately, first beam down one, try the mission (or battle, etc.), and if they get stopped then beam down another team, etc. The only exception is the case when one player beams down Away Teams from different affiliations and no treaty is in effect that allows them to be intermixed. In that case they are separate Away Teams in the same place.

Q: If my Away Team gets stopped by not overcoming a dilemma and then I use Emergency Transporter Armbands to beam them back to the ship, do they become unstopped?

A: No. There is nothing in the game presently that will "unstop" anything, (except for the Distortion of Space/Time Continuum that allows a ship and its crew to "make another move."

Q : Does the Away Team have to theoretically be able to complete the mission in order to be allowed to attempt the mission?

A : No. You can attempt the mission even if the Away Team theoretically can't complete it. If they make it through the dilemmas, they won't be able to go any further; but later you might bring the cards there that can actually complete the mission.

Q : Can an Away Team "abort" a Mission before going through every dilemma at a certain location?

A : If your Away Team gets stopped, it can't continue this turn and next turn you can choose to either continue or beam up and try again later. However, once you commit an Away Team to attempting a mission, you can't suddenly change your mind in mid-stream and beam up even though the Away Team hasn't been stopped by the first dilemma it met. The idea of the dilemma is that they represent the unknowns, the plot twists that come up when you enter the adventure of transporting to the planet. Once you are started, you are committed.

Also, to allow this would introduce a possibility for cheating, by peeking at the next dilemma.

Q: What constitutes an "Away Team" for a Space Mission?

A: The Away Team for a Space Mission is the entire crew of the ship (or the crew of the outpost). This means you might be exposing valuable personnel that you would rather not.

Q: Can crew members located on different ships be designated as on the same Away Team for a Space Mission?

A: Crews from two different ships cannot normally be combined to constitute a single "Away Team" crew for space missions. Beam the people you want to be involved in the mission to one ship, and beam the ones you don't want involved to the other. Note that the two crews can be used separately as two separate crews, trying the mission with one crew, and if they get stopped then trying it with the other crew.

Borg

(The Borg Ship, Rogue Borg)

Q: Does the Borg Ship really attack *everything*?

A: When it first appears, it attacks "everything and anything" in space at that location. When it moves to the next location, it attacks everything and anything there. If during a turn a player moves a ship to where the Borg Ship is and stops there, the Borg Ship attacks it. However, you can fly past the Borg Ship by going over it, which is the main method of getting out of its way. The Borg Ship attacks *each* individual thing in space at that location.

Q: Are cloaked ships immune to the Borg Ship?

A: If a ship has a cloaking device that is already activated when it encounters the Borg Ship, it will be safe. Some have argued that the Borg are advanced enough to discover cloaked ships, but there is no support for that in the series. Note that when doing a Planet Mission a ship must decloak before beaming down the Away Team. Ships can only cloak/decloak once per turn, so if the Away Team hits a Borg Ship dilemma the ship might still be uncloaked and vulnerable. Also note that a cloaked ship located with a Borg Ship will be attacked if for some reason it loses its cloak. There are other means of dealing with Borg Ships besides cloaking, such as using Hugh.

Q: How can you destroy a Borg Ship to earn the Bonus?

A: If you attack it with several ships, you might have enough firepower to damage it (you need weapons of more than 24 total). Of course, these ships will each be attacked by the Borg Ship as well. The damaged Borg Ship is turned upside down to indicate damage. If it is damaged twice, it is destroyed. The player who bags it gets the big 45 point bonus.

Q: Is the Borg Ship affected by Where No One Has Gone Before or other Interrupt or Event cards?

A: The correct ruling is the Borg Ship is a Dilemma card—not a *ship* per se—so it is *not* affected by various Interrupt or Event cards which are *played on a ship*, such as Temporal Rift, Transwarp Conduit, and Loss of Orbital Stability. However, the Borg Ship does *move* like a ship, and thus it *is* affected by

Interrupts and Events that are "in space" which it encounters, such as the Tetryon Field, and Subspace Warp Rift. Some of these have little effect, but others do have interesting effects—particularly Where No One Has Gone Before, Q-Net, and Wormholes.

Q: Is there a limit to the number of Borg Ships that can be in play?

A: Yes, in the sense that the game has built-in limitations and defenses. The Borg Ship is a Space Dilemma and thus there can at most be one per Space Mission. But any number of them can be activated and on the move at any given time.

Q: When Rogue Borg have taken over a ship and Lore Returns is in play, can they be beamed down to a planet to battle enemy Away Teams?

A: Yes.

Card Symbols

Q: If the card states something like, "Unless Science and Cunning >35...." Does that mean Science >35 *and* Cunning >35 or the combination of the two >35?

A: This example translates as, "Unless you have one Science Personnel and a total amount of Cunning greater than 35...." These symbols are not boolean algebra, they refer to Attributes (Strength, Cunning, Integrity for the Personnel, or Weapons, Shields, and Range for the Ships), and state how much of that attribute you need. They don't refer to Classifications or Skills of Personnel. Sometimes they might seem a little ambiguous, but only if you read them algebraically. If a card calls for more than one Personnel classification or skill it will say, "2 Science" or "3 Diplomacy," which means you need at least that many Personnel with those skills.

Cloaked Ships

Q: Can Events and Interrupts be played on a cloaked ship?

A: Generally speaking, these cards *can* be played on a cloaked ship, as long as the card is "logically independent of cloaking ability." Most Events and Interrupts are "acts of nature" or "accidental encounters" of some sort that happen to the ship independently of cloaking ability, not something invoked by the opponent. For example, a Plasma Fire can happen aboard a ship whether it is cloaked or not, (even if your opponent can't technically see the ship) and thus this card can be played on a cloaked ship.

However, Event or Interrupt cards which represent the actions of the opponent that would logically be frustrated by cloaking should not be playable on a cloaked ship. For example, a Scan card doesn't make sense to play since a cloaked ship cannot be scanned, by definition. This distinction is usually obvious from the card, using some *Star Trek* sense.

Q: Can you cloak and uncloak (or vice versa) both in the span of one round?

A: No, you can only do one per turn for each ship.

Q: Do you have to uncloak to attempt a Space Mission?

A: Yes, a ship must be uncloaked to try the mission (unless you have a special card that allows otherwise). A ship under cloak expends a lot of energy which is assumed to interfere with the ability to achieve the mission requirements at a space location.

Q: Is it possible to cloak a damaged ship?

A: No.

Q: Can a ship enter play at an outpost already cloaked?

A: A ship can't be put into play at the outpost already cloaked, because there is nobody aboard to push the cloak button. What you can do, however, is dock the ship at the outpost normally, immediately move everyone aboard, and then cloak the ship. This has almost the same effect.

Q: Can Rogue Borg be played upon a cloaked ship?

A: The current ruling on this is that there is no canonical evidence in the show that the Borg have the technology to detect cloaked ships; therefore, the Rogue Borg can't be used on a cloaked ship. Since the Rogue Borg are Interrupts, just wait until the ship decloaks and then attack it.

Dilemmas

Q: What does it mean to "overcome" a dilemma?

A: The rule to go by in "overcoming" dilemmas, therefore, is as follows:

(1) Dilemma cards with no "conditions" are automatically "overcome"—they have their effect, but do not "stop" the Away Team.

(2) Cards which do have conditions will "stop" the Away Team and have their effect unless you "overcome" the dilemma by meeting those conditions, (this all assumes the Dilemma card itself doesn't override this rule, such as the Alien Parasites Dilemma card).

Q: If there is more than one ship present at a location when a space mission is being attempted and the Dilemma card says, "Play on ship" (like Junior, see above), to which ship does this apply?

A: Dilemma cards in such situations normally apply to the ship that was the one attempting the mission, unless otherwise stated.

Q: What does "Discard Dilemma" on several of the Dilemma cards mean?

A: (1) Most Dilemma cards will have their "plot-twist effect" and then go away. The words "Discard dilemma" simply remind you to discard the Dilemma after it is used—whether or not you were able to overcome its conditions.

(2) However, several Dilemma cards are more "permanent" in nature. They are not discarded until you overcome them. For example, the "Impassable Door" is a simple dilemma that stays in place until you bring up the Computer Skill to meet the conditions of getting past it. Such cards as this do

not say "Discard Dilemma." They remain in place until someone overcomes them.

(3) There are a few Dilemma cards that "enter the game" so to speak; such as ones which are "Played on your ship," like Junior, which attaches itself to your ship and starts sucking out its energy. Dilemmas like this are no longer in effect at the mission location. (Someone else trying the mission won't be affected by them.) But they are still in effect as described on the card. For example, Junior stays on your ship until you meet the conditions of removing him as described on the card, or until the ship is destroyed.

Q: The rules state, "Players may not place duplicate Dilemma or Artifact cards at the same location. If found, duplicate cards are simply discarded." Does this refer to duplicate cards played to the same location by one player, or any duplicate created when both players happen to play the same dilemma at one location?

A: This refers to *both* players. *Any* duplicates, regardless of who played it, are discarded when they are found.

Q: Can you send down a single person to attempt a mission, sacrificing him to see what the first dilemma is?

A: Yes, the "red shirt" strategy is a major tactic and certainly is allowed. There is a risk to it, however, because some dilemmas have powerfully negative effects that are relatively easy to overcome. Yet, if you "red shirt" such a dilemma, you will release very undesirable consequences!

Q: Is the Tsiolkovsky Infection dilemma cumulative? Since it stays on the ship, could the same ship encounter more than one?

A: No. If you run into another one, it is still only affecting your first-listed skill. You can only become affected once—the infection is either "on" or "off."

Q: The Tsiolkovsky Infection causes affected cards to "lose their first-listed skill." If this is a super-skill, like Diplomacy x3, does the character lose it all, or just part of it?

A: The character loses all of it. The "Diplomacy x3" is not three diplomacy skills, it refers to a large amount of that skill.

Docking Ships

Q: When a new ship comes into play at the outpost, can it move that same turn?

A: Yes it can, as long as you move the necessary people aboard to staff the ship properly.

End of Turn

Q: What is the definition of the "end of turn," which is a phrase often used on the cards, such as "...ship explodes at end of your turn?"

A: Anything that happens at the "end of turn" is the "last thing you do before the card draw." As the rules say, you "signal the end of your turn" when you draw your card. In other words, when the card is drawn, the turn is completely over. So, something at the end of a turn happens just before the turn is over. If several things are scheduled to happen at the end of a particular turn, take them in any sequence.

Equipment

Q: How do Equipment cards like the Engineering Kit work?

A : They multiply skills on crews and Away Teams. For example, an Engineering Kit turns every Officer at that location into an Engineer as well. Thus, skillful use of Equipment can create a very strong Away Team. For instance, if you had an Away Team with 4 Officers, 1 Engineering Kit, and 1 Medi-Kit, you essentially would have 4 Officer, 4 Engineer, and 4 Medical personnel in the Away Team, using just six cards.

Q : If an Away Team with equipment gets wiped out, is the equipment destroyed as well?

A : The equipment normally would not be destroyed, and thus would be left on the planet, where the owner of the equipment could later go and retrieve it. The opponent cannot retrieve them, because theoretically he would not know where to find them on the planet. This is one of the advantages of using Equipment cards—they aren't as vulnerable as Personnel.

Q : If there is no treaty in effect, can affiliation-specific Equipment like a Romulan Disruptor be "handled" by the other affiliations?

A : Anybody, anytime, can move or beam equipment around, because they are "things." It's just that in game terms only certain affiliations can actually use that equipment as stated on the individual cards.

Q: What if there is a treaty in effect—can my Federation people use the Romulan Disruptor?

A: If there is a treaty, then both affiliations can use the equipment, because under a treaty the allied affiliations share their cards "as if they were one affiliation." You might rationalize that they teach each other how to use the equipment.

Q: Are equipment effects transferrable? For example, the Engineering Kit says, "Gives all of your Officer-classification personnel the extra skill of Engineer where present." So, my Officer now acts as an Engineer, too. But what if I now add a Tricorder which says, "Gives all of your Engineer-classification personnel the extra skill of Science where present." Does that mean my Officer/Engineer now acts as a Scientist as well?

A: No, the equipment only enhances the "classification" as a new skill. You might think of it as a "temporary ability," but it doesn't transfer.

Q: Do "super-Engineers" benefit twice from Equipment cards? For example, Geordi LaForge is a Super-Engineer with an Engineer classification and extra Engineer skill. If he is with a Tricorder (which gives Science skill to Engineer-classification personnel), would he also have double Science skill?

A: No. The cards refer only to the "classification" of the personnel.

Q: A Phaser says "each personnel Strength +2 where present." Does each member of the Away Team get +2, or only one member per phaser?

A: Wherever a phaser is present, everyone on the Away Team gets the +2. If you have two phasers, you get +4.

Exhausted Deck

Q: What happens if you run out of cards to draw?

A: As soon as either player's deck runs out, the game is over and the player who then has the highest score wins the game. This is important since one major tactic is to try to exhaust one of the player's draw decks whenever you are leading the game on points.

Gaps in Normal Space

Q: Do gaps in normal space create a new spaceline location?

A: Essentially, yes. You place it between one of the spaceline locations, where it creates a new location with a span of four across it. Anything stopping there gets a crewmember killed, so you have to "fly over" it. It can be destroyed by Kevin Uxbridge.

Horga'hn

Q: The Horga'hn card says that it "allows" you to take two turns—is this optional?

A: Yes, it says you are allowed to, not that you "must." You could only take the normal one turn if you want to.

Holodeck

Q: Does a Holoprojector work whether or not you have a ship with a holodeck?

A: Yes, the Holoprojector is sort of like a portable Holodeck installed on all your ships at the same time, but with the advantage that it allows your holocharacter personnel to not only be used on ships, but to be used on planets as well.

Q: Can Fek'lhr be played on a Federation ship with a holodeck?

A: Despite being a holocharacter, Fek'lhr is a Klingon personnel. Klingons normally won't travel on Federation ships due to a mismatch of affiliations so normally he can't be used on a

Federation ship. Even though any holodeck can theoretically create anything, unless there is a treaty in place the Federation doesn't have a program for Fek'lhr to use. However, if a Federation/Klingon Treaty is in effect, then each affiliation's holocharacter programs are shared just like everything else, and thus Fek'lhr could be used on a Federation holodeck under treaty.

Intruders

(Alien Parasites, Alien Probe, Telepathic Kidnappers)

Q: The Alien Parasites card says the opponent gets to "control" my ship's crew until stopped. Can he/she deliberately endanger the crew? Can he/she attempt a mission and, if successful, score it for himself?

A: The Alien Parasites card says: "Unless Integrity >32, Away Team infected. They beam back and opponent immediately controls ship and crew until stopped." Then turn resumes. This is a somewhat exceptional card, of course, so it is a little broadly worded. But basically it means that if you don't have the integrity, the opponent gets to do with your ship and the crew whatever he wants, using "legal" moves. Think of it as if a madman has taken over your crew.

The opponent has many options of things he can do with the ship. If the ship still has movement range available, it can still be moved somewhere. It can be used to start a battle, or beam crew members off to strand them on planets the ship passes. The opponent can attempt a mission at a location where he knows they will not be able to overcome the dilemma, and thus will experience negative effects. The current ruling is that if the opponent attempts and completes a mission with them it will score for him. This continues until he/she is finished or until the ship and crew involved are all stopped.

Q: Should the killer combination of the Telepathic Kidnappers and Alien Probe cards be outlawed?

A: It isn't necessarily easy to get the two into play—you have to stock your deck for it, have the cards come up, and then take two turns getting them down. Your opponent has options in the meantime—a savvy player can stock his deck with defenses for this strategy.

Are you sure it is a total "killer"? The Alien Probe makes both players play with cards exposed. The Telepathic Alien Kidnappers says, "At end of each turn, guess a card type and point to a card in your opponent's hand.

Card must be shown. If guessed correctly, card is discarded." Thus, while it is true that each turn you can zap any one of the opponent's cards (which is indeed powerful), you do *not* have control over the card he draws that turn. Remember the above-listed definition of "end of turn," it happens *just before* the card draw. Then, the card the opponent draws will be safe. If the opponent draws a Kevin Uxbridge, for example, he/she can immediately use it to destroy one of the Events.

Even if this card-combo becomes too powerful and player consensus rises against using it, Decipher would prefer to handle the situation naturally rather than through an artificial rule. A new card in the next expansion set could be created to mitigate or destroy such a tactic. In the meantime, you can always play with a house rule against this combination if you feel you must.

Q: Are the Telepathic Alien Kidnappers cumulative? It doesn't say either way on the card.

A: Yes, and for those who are planning to use this strategy, future cards in the next expansion will be affecting the T.A.Kidnappers.

Leadership

Q: How does Leadership work? Are all Officers leaders or are only people with Leadership leaders?

A: The concepts of Leader and Leadership are related but slightly different in the game. In terms of Battles, you need to have a Leader to fight offensively. A Leader for Battles is any Officer or anyone with Leadership listed as a skill. Leadership, however, can also be required by missions or dilemmas, etc. In this case, the cards refer to the *skill* of Leadership, not to just any old Officer. Thus, to meet a "Leadership" requirement for a mission you need at least one personnel with the special *skill* of Leadership listed in his/her skills box.

Think of it this way: All Officers go to military academies where they learn how to battle. So they all have the ability to lead in battle (indeed, this is one of the purposes of officers in the game). But not all of them have the charisma to be *skilled* at Leadership in a more general way such as Captain Picard or Admiral Nechayev.

Q: Why does Toral have only "1/2 Leadership" skill?

A: Toral was a young and honorless illegitimate son of Duras who tried to become Leader of the Klingon High Council and failed, so he has only 1/2 Leadership. His weak Leadership is sufficient to count as being a Leader for a battle, but it is *not* sufficient for the Leadership requirement listed on a Mission or Dilemma card—you must have full Leadership skill for those. If you ever get him together with somebody else with 1/2 Leadership, you'll have 1 full Leadership.

Love Interests

Q: Can you rescue your crewman who has gone off with the alien of the opposite sex without beaming down to the planet with an Away Team?

A: Yes. You can go to that planet and just beam him/her up. By then, the subject has come to his/her senses, and returns to the crew.

Q: Is Data affected by the Male's Love Interest dilemma? What cards are *not* affected by Male/Female Love Interest?

A : Only personnel which are "asexual" (without sex) are not affected by the Love Interest dilemmas. This includes mainly Exocomps, but also Soren (who is androgynous, although she did show some female feelings, but these were suppressed). This immunity is one nice advantage of such characters.

Data, even though he is an android, is considered to be a male, and thus susceptible to the Male's Love Interest. He is described in the series as a "fully functional" male, (as Tasha Yar can attest). He is, therefore, a male in terms of the gameplay. The series has shown him many times being swayed and affected by women—he's had more girl-friends than Geordi!

Menthar Booby Trap

Q : How does the Menthar Booby Trap work?

A : This Space Dilemma card says: "Unless Medical present, one crew member killed (random selection). Ship can't move until 2 Engineer present." This means it has two effects. First, one of the crew will be killed unless you have a Medical personnel present. Second, the ship can't move unless you have two Engineers there. In the latter case, the ship will be "stuck" there forever until it can be rescued. You can rescue it by bringing the necessary Engineers there in another ship. If you can't do that, you can at least bring up another ship and beam the crew off the trapped ship. Note that the first effect comes first—if you have two Engineers but no Medical aboard, one of the Engineers might get killed before they can free the ship in step 2! Other ships coming to this location are not affected by the Trap. A ship caught in a Menthar Booby Trap *can* participate in a battle if one comes its way.

Moving Personnel

Q: Can you "ferry" personnel down the spaceline with several ships?

A: Yes. Clever manipulation of ships can give you lots of movement freedom.

Q: Can two ships passing each other beam personnel between themselves (if they are your own ships)?

A: Yes.

Personnel Classifications

Q: What are the capitalized skills on the Personnel cards, like Engineer?

A: Some "classifications" like Science, Medical, etc. can appear in a character's skill box, if the character has special professional-level skills in that area in addition to the normal classification. An Engineer with Engineer also listed in his skill box (like Geordi LaForge) is essentially a "super-Engineer" (or "double-Engineer"), and would count as 2 Engineers. A Scientist who also has Medical listed as a skill (like Vekor) essentially counts as both, etc. All of this is a way of more accurately reflecting the abilities of those characters who are especially skillful in one area or skillful in more than one area, like Data and Geordi.

Q: Do you need to have a non-aligned Personnel onboard a non-aligned ship to meet that ship's staffing requirements?

A: Personnel of any affiliation can be used to meet its staffing requirements.

Plasma Fire

Q: If Plasma Fire continues to damage a ship every turn, does that mean it destroys a ship in two rounds or just keeps it in a "damaged" state until Security puts it out?

A: The ship gets damaged by the Plasma Fire at the end of each of your turns, beginning at the end of your next turn. ("Damage" here means normal ship damage, like battle damage.) Thus, normally if it is not extinguished the ship is a goner in two turns. However, there is the chance the player might be able to repair the ship, thus keeping it alive longer, or bring the Security in the meantime.

Q-Net

Q: Can a Q2 get rid of a Q-Net?

A: No. Q2 can only interfere with Q-related dilemmas. However, since the Q-Net is an Event, it can be destroyed by Kevin Uxbridge.

Red Alert

Q: After the Red Alert is in play, allowing you to play as many Ship, Personnel, or Equipment as desired each turn, do these cards count as your normal card play or can you also play, say, an Event?

A: Once the Red Alert card is in play, (after the initial turn) a group of cards played under a Red Alert count as your normal card play during any turn. If you want to play an Event, you can't play any Red Alert cards that turn.

Rescuing a Crew

Q: If my ship is about to be destroyed, can I save the crew, such as by beaming them down to a planet?

A: Yes, if your ship is going to be destroyed, you can try to save the crew by beaming them down to a planet first, where they will be stranded but can be picked up later. (They would be vulnerable to attack there from enemy Away Teams.) The only time you can't do this is in the middle of a ship-to-ship battle (where there is logically not enough time to escape this way). There is an Interrupt card, however, called Emergency Transporter Armbands, that does allow such a means of escape even during a battle. Note that a crew can also escape by using an Escape Pod card, as well as other ways.

Res-Q and Palor Toff

Q: When using cards like Res-Q or Palor Toff to regenerate a card, does the card go into your hand or into play?

A: The card goes into your hand (unless otherwise stated).

Q: Can Res-Q or Palor Toff regenerate a Dilemma card?

A: Theoretically you can—however at the present time there is no way to use a Dilemma card in your hand, so there would be no point to it. Dilemma cards are only used during the seed phase. (It is likely, however, that we will have a card in a future expansion set that allows later use of dilemmas.)

Shields

Q: When an outpost extends its shields to a ship in its space, are the outpost's shields reduced?

A: No.

Q: Is the shield extended to all its ships in orbit?

A: Yes.

Static Warp Bubble

Q: What is the official answer on the use of this card—does the discard happen before or after the draw?

A: The discard happens anytime *before* you draw, (the card draw signifies the end of your turn, so the discard must happen before then). This way, you will always have at least one card in hand to play with even if it drains you all the way down. If you have one card left and it is your turn, you can play that card during your turn. At the end of your turn you have no cards left to discard, but still get your card draw to actually end your turn.

Q: Is this a killer card? By forcing your opponent to discard every round, how can it be countered?

A: A Static Warp Bubble is fairly easy to overcome. Kevin Uxbridge will eliminate it entirely and The Traveler: Transcendence counters it. It is no doubt a pretty strong card, but not a killer even if you can't get rid of it.

Q: It says the player must discard a card. Could this include discarding a card that is already in play on the table, or does it refer only to cards in your hand?

A: Only to cards in your hand.

Supernova

Q: Does a Supernova destroy a Particle Fountain?

A: It destroys the card along with all other cards there, but not the points earned by the person who played it. At the present time there is no way to take away points that have been earned by a player. Take the particle fountain and set it aside with other bonus point cards to keep the score indicated.

Tractor Beams

Q: How is this Ship attribute used?

A: Currently there are two uses for it, and there may be more in the future. There is an Interrupt card called "Ship Seizure" which allows ships with Tractor Beams to tow away (i.e. destroy) an opponent's empty ship. Also, the Radioactive Garbage Scow is a dilemma that blocks a mission until you have a ship with tractor beams tow it out of the way—and leave it somewhere else.

Warp Speed

Q: Is a ship's Range the same as its Warp Speed?

A: You can think of it that way, but technically Range is just distance. Remember that the spaceline is a one-dimensional representation of a 3-dimensional universe, and the *time* of a turn is unclear, so calculation of *speed* here has little meaning. It is better to define range, therefore, as just how far you can go in a turn, not how fast.

Information for Collectors

Collectors are always interested in the "stats" of a product like this, which helps them assess which cards are most powerful or most valuable, etc. Here are some basic stats on the game as of this writing:

Editions / Print Run Size / Availability

First Printing:
Limited Edition (black border)
45,900,000 cards
Released Nov. 7, 1994

Second Printing:
Unlimited Edition (white border)
45,900,000 cards
Released December, 1994

Third Printing:
Unlimited Edition (white border)
162,000,000 cards
Released early February, 1995

Fourth Printing — "Beta"
Unlimited Edition (white border)
Quantity unknown
Scheduled for Summer, 1995

This edition will have some new features of interest to collectors. Decipher is taking the opportunity to revise the initial cards with some minor changes to fix a half dozen typos (three of which are the consistently misspelled name "Lwaxanna Troi," which appears on three cards, it should have one "n"), to improve the wording of a few other cards which are considered to be unclear or inaccurate, and a few other minor things. (A listing of the exact changes is available on the Internet). You will be able to identify the "beta" set from the earlier "alpha" set by the copyright date on the side of each box. Alpha sets are 1994, beta sets are 1995.

Collector's Tin
Special Edition (one of each card)
$100 SRP
Scheduled release: Spring, 1995

The "Two-Player Introductory Game"

Scheduled for Summer 1995, this is a specially packaged edition with pre-selected cards for 2 players playable "right out of the box." It has a Federation deck and a Klingon deck, each made up of common cards as well as 20 brand new cards created specially for this set. It will be an excellent "quick and easy" introduction for newcomers, including some alternate simplified rules to help them get started.

Black Border (Limited) vs. White Border (Unlimited)

Decipher's policy (for the initial set as well as the expansion sets) is to first produce them in a black-border edition, which will be of limited quantity. Thereafter, those cards will be available in white border only; no more black border sets will be produced. This format is for the benefit of both collectors and players. The black borders, because they are limited and relatively scarce, become the cards of highest value, and tend to be hoarded.

White border cards are mostly for players, since they are less scarce (although many of them are still valuable on the secondary market and are often traded as well).

Expansion sets will be released in the same format — first black border, followed by unlimited white border. Furthermore, cards which are first produced and distributed in other ways, such as in the Two-Player Introductory Game, the Warp Packs, or various "Premium" promotional cards or "Ultra-Rare" cards, will usually be provided in black-border editions as soon as possible, for the benefit of black-border collectors who want to complete their set.

Other than border color, there is no difference between the cards in limited or unlimited editions, and there is no differency in the frequency of their occurence.

Card Rarity and Frequency

Of the 363 cards in the initial set, 121 are rare, 121 are uncommon, and 121 are common. None of these are duplicated, so each of the 121 rare cards is equally rare, etc. The cards are then packaged in a pure random assorting method, with no secondary sorting or other tricks to make certain cards more rare.

In each 60-card Starter Set there are:

45 Common cards (75%)

13 Uncommon cards (21.67%)

2 Rare cards (3.33%)

In each 15-card Expansion Pack there are:

11 Common cards (73.33%)

3 Uncommon cards (20%)

1 Rare card (6.67%)

Card Stock

The ST:TNG CCG cards are printed on a thick card stock called superlux—the top quality available. The cards are coated to what is called casino-quality slippage for easy play and durability, and feature American-style rounded corners. The printing is done with 175-point line screens — again the highest quality the printer could provide.

Ultra-Rare Cards

Decipher plans the release of several unusual "ultra-rare" cards, which will be "ultra cool" highly desirable cards that are released in very limited runs as part of various promotions. Distribution of these special cards will be handled in a special way to

nsure fairness to everyone who is interested. To find out the latest about ultra-rares
and how you can get involved, please con-
sult Decipher's information sources.

Card "Lore" and Sources

Each card contains some interesting background information about what it portrays,
called its "lore." This information was
researched from many sources, and was
authorized and authenticated by Paramount.
Sources of "canonical" information were
The Star Trek Encyclopedia (by Michael
Okuda, Denise Okuda, and Debbie Mirek;
Pocket Books, 1994), plus extensive
research of the television series itself, and
official help from the experts at Paramount.

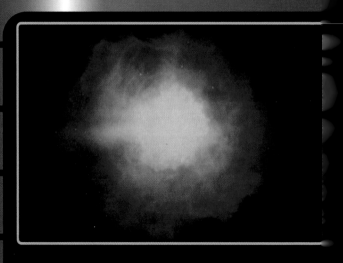

Expansion Plans

The expandability of ST:TNG CCG is one of its strengths. The creation of new cards, and new *kinds* of cards constantly keeps the play fresh and exciting—allowing for the exploration of new corners of the *Star Trek* universe. Having worked on these expansion sets for months now, it never fails to amaze me how much potential for expansion there actually is. The initial set of 363 cards that introduced ST:TNG CCG is just the beginning!

Beginning mid-1995, Decipher will start shipping expansion sets for ST:TNG CCG. All the cards in the expansion sets will play with the existing universe of cards, but some cards will add new elements to the gameplay. The first three expansion sets will contain approximately 120 cards each. Here is some basic information on the first three expansions:

Alternate Universe

The first expansion set will be titled "Alternate Universe." About twenty-five to thirty percent of these cards will be people and things which appeared in *The Next Generation*, but were "not from this universe" (i.e. from time travel, other dimensions, fantasies, illusions, etc.). They are thus a separate category of cards and will be marked with a special icon.

Logically, such people or things would not normally interact with "real" people from the show. A way to bring them together is needed. This expansion set will introduce a new kind of card called a "linking card." To get from the Alternate Universe to the "real" one of the main game, they link through a linking card, in this case via the Alternate Universe Door card (which functions like a permanent Event card). Such linking cards will also come into play for other expansions or when linking to other series. You will learn more about this concept in the future.

The rest of this expansion set will deepen the ST:TNG CCG universes with more missions, events, dilemmas, interrupts, etc. providing more variety, player interaction, and balance to the existing card types. It will also provide some elements that counter-balance cards which, for one reason or another, players presently feel are too strong.

The expansion set will be sold in 15-card expansion packs. Each pack will have a small sheet of paper briefly mentioning noteworthy rule-related points about the new cards. Hopefully this combined with the wording of the cards themselves will make their uses clear, but as usual if there are any questions brought out by the new cards they will be answered through "Frequently Asked Questions" (FAQs) posted on Decipher's information sources.

Q-Continuum

Next, approximately three to four months later, is planned for the "Q-Continuum" expansion. As you might guess, a large per-centage of these cards will involve Q-related mischief of various kinds, sometimes rather on the wild side, including the possibility of a "side-game" which is played "inside" the existing game (the way Q was often kidnap-ping Picard and Company to play games during the series).

Holodeck

Three to four months after that, you will see a third expansion set titled "Holodeck Adventures." Holographic re-creations were "introduced" in the initial set, but only to a minor extent. The first expansions will also provide additional holographic stuff, but this expansion set will feature this aspect of the game and develop it much further! This set will also contain some new gameplay elements and a new linking card—a Holodeck Door. Almost anything is possible in a holodeck!

Tie-Ins with Star Trek Books

Many people have asked if characters from the many popular *Star Trek* novels, short stories, etc. will be used in the game. The answer is no. Such characters are not considered official by Paramount. Also, there are no video or photographic images for such characters, which are necessary to maintain the same "look" throughout the entire universe of ST:TNG CCG cards.

Popular Advance Variations

The open-ended and free-form play of ST:TNG CCG naturally allows for experimenting with variations to suit the gameplay tastes of players, the length of play, and other elements of the game. Experimenting with play variations is part of the fun!

One simple way people do this is to create "house rules" that they play with among their play group. House rules usually include either restricting use of certain cards that the group doesn't like, or creating alternate ways to enhance certain cards in addition to the official way. Such house rules are fine for play with friends, but remember that if you go to play in tournaments or with other players outside your own group, people will not use those same house rules, and confusion may result. However, there are a number of "advanced variations" that enhance or extend certain elements of the game. Some of these are listed in the rulebook, and others have been suggested by players.

These advanced variations are still somewhat in a state of flux. Eventually they will become more formalized as they evolve. Look for the latest information on Decipher's information sources like decipher.com.

Variation #1:
Long Spacelines and Larger Decks

Playing with a long spaceline is a nice change of pace—giving you the feeling of "infinite" space. This variation tends to take a lot longer to play, but if you prefer a long game, it allows you to bring out fleets of ships, create long-term strategies, and get into major battles.

When you do this, it is considered best to enlarge the size of your total deck and the final winning score accordingly, to keep the same basic proportions.

Whenever you double the size of the deck as in this case, there is a big question of how many Dilemma cards the player is allowed. In the standard game, you can have up to half your deck taken up by seed cards, giving you as many as 24 dilemmas to place. If you play with a deck of 120 cards, however, this rule means you can have 54 dilemmas to place. There are ways around situations in which the opponent piles up dilemmas at your locations. Theoretically, keeping the rule of half the deck for seed cards works for any size.

Some players, however, play with the rule that the number of dilemmas you can have in your deck when playing with larger decks should have the same proportion relative to the number of missions that the standard game has. The standard game has 12 Spaceline cards and each player at most can have 24 Dilemmas. That is two dilemmas per mission for each player. And they maintain this proportion for whatever the size of spaceline they play with.

Variation #2:
No Duplication in the Universe

This variation gives a slightly different flavor to the play. In the standard game, if both players have stocked the same cards, it is okay if players bring out the same cards—you are only restricted from bringing out more than one yourself, such as having two Captain Picards on your side at once. Under the "no duplication in the universe" rule, however, duplications are not allowed on *either* side.

For example, if your opponent introduces Lieutenant Worf into play, you will not be allowed to play this card, as long as your opponent's Lieutenant Worf card remains in play. This is not only a little more realistic, but also has some interesting effects for strategy. If you and your opponent happen to have stocked cards of similar Affiliations, there will be a race to get key cards into play first!

Variation #3:
Random Seeding of Dilemma Cards

A third popular variation involves play in which the Dilemma cards are seeded randomly instead of intentionally by the players.

1) Create the spaceline as usual.

2) Each player takes their dilemma cards, and divides them into space and planet dilemma piles.

3) Player A shuffles his/her Space Dilemma cards and randomly places them (without looking) under the Space Mission cards, one under each mission, starting at either end of the spaceline and going across, until they are gone.

4) Player B does the same, starting at the other end of the spaceline.

5) Player B does the same with the planet dilemmas, placing them one at a time under Planet Missions, starting at either end of the spaceline until they are gone.

6) Player A does the same with planet dilemmas, starting at the other end of the spaceline.

The result is that the spaceline gets seeded somewhat randomly and evenly across the line, creating more of a surprise factor.

Multi-Player Variations

Multi-player ST:TNG CCG play (allowing for 3, 4, or more players) has also proven to be popular. Some even prefer it to the two-player game.

When playing with three or more players, you must adapt the game by treating the spaceline differently and interpreting the cards for multi-player use. Most cards translate well for multiple players using common sense—but some require some re-interpretation. For example, a card that refers to "the far end of the spaceline" can be unclear if an unusually shaped spaceline is being used which might have more than one end.

It might be interpreted as referring to either end in that case. Agree on ways to translate such cards. Many variations for more than two players are being proposed and tested by fans of the game, especially on the Internet. These range from simple team versions (in which for example four players play using partnerships of two, combining their efforts), to complex systems involving two-dimensional spacelines laid out in a grid-like patterns, upon which the ships can move vertically as well as horizontally. The more complex versions of these are still under development and require some experience to play (because keeping track of who owns what cards can be difficult). For the latest information on them as they evolve, check Decipher's information sources like decipher.com.

Two other popular systems, however, require only minor changes in the spaceline, and are so far more popular—the "Y-System" and the "Triangle System."

Variation #1:
The "Y" and "+" Systems
(3 or 4 players)

This variation was suggested by several players, apparently first by Tim Grasso in *Conjure* magazine. It seems to be the most popular multi-player variation so far, and works smoothly for 3 or 4 players.

It plays essentially the same way as the standard two-player game, but uses a clever way of doing the spaceline that emulates two-player while accommodating 3 or 4.

For three players, you create the spaceline using a "Y" shape on the table, looking something like this:

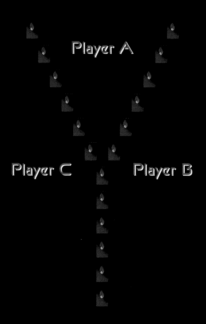

Player A

Player C   Player B

Each player sits in one of the three "areas" using the spaceline as the boundary between them and the other two players, as shown in this diagram. Nathan Erwin suggests the players agree to each play a different affiliation, one of each, for maximum effect.

Players move their ships along their own side of the two lines of the "Y" that face them. Player B shares six cards (to the left) in common with Player C, and six cards in common (to the right) with Player A. Player B can move ships back and forth on his or her side of those 12 cards. Player B normally cannot move to the other line of cards (the boundary between A & C).

Variation: Players can move onto the opposing players' shared spaceline with Wormholes or by using Where No One Has Gone Before (which allows you to go off one end and come on either of the other two ends). Another idea is to treat the intersection of the three lines as a "neutral zone" at which any ship can be located, and from which it can pass onto the other spaceline spokes.

For four players, use a "+" shape for the spaceline, with four "sectors" of control. For five players, use an 5-pointed star shape, etc.

Variation #2:
"Triangle" and "Square" Approach
(3 or more players)

This variation was first proposed by T2Thomas@aol.com and Voquih@netcom.com. It uses a spaceline in the shape of a triangle (three players). The description here is for three, but four works the same using a square setup, five with a pentagonal setup, six with a hexagon, etc.

Each player plays six mission cards to build a triangular spaceline that looks something like this:

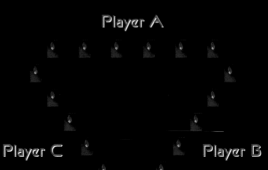

In this variation, players play along their own side of the spaceline. Movement around to the other sides of the spaceline can be done in two ways:

1) Move from the "outside track" on your side to the "inside tracks" of the opponent's lines.

2) Play a Where No One Has Gone Before on the appropriate intersection. You can use Wormholes (which are considered "stable wormholes") to get to someone else's spaceline. After the wormholes are used, they stay where they are, allowing free use of them for the duration of the game. A house rule should then be established that, along with the 60 card deck, each player must have 1 Where No One Has Gone Before, and 2 Wormholes for each player playing beyond the first, (i.e. 2 Where No One Has Gone Before cards and 4 Wormholes for a 3-player game).

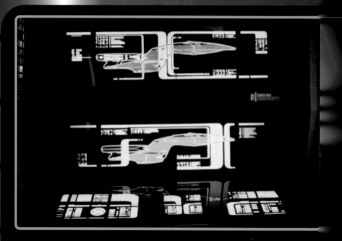

Sources of Information

The *Star Trek: The Next Generation: Customizable Card Game* is a game system which is constantly evolving. As new cards come out, they change the evaluation of earlier cards, creating new uses and new strategies. To "expand your power in the universe" you need to keep up with the latest information on the game.

Decipher has set up a number of sources of information. One of them is the line of Player's Guide books which discuss the details of strategies for the cards and the expansion sets. In addition, there are other public sources of free information you can access.

The Internet

For those with computer modem access to the information highway, there are many terrific sources of information, as well as places to discuss the game and propose trades. You can download all the rules "FAQs" (frequently asked questions), get card lists, pictures, announcements of upcoming products and release dates, sneak previews of new cards, etc.

The main site for such information is decipher.com, Decipher's own Internet site. If you have ftp access, you can download files by connecting to "ftp.decipher.com". If you have www access, you can browse their web site—"http://decipher.com/decipher" with any web browser (Mosaic, Netscape, Lynx, etc).

E-Mail

If you only have e-mail access, you can get info and participate in game discussions via "ListServ" Mailing Lists. For more information about this, contact DAnswerMan@decipher.com.

You can always get help with your questions by e-mail to:

DAnswerMan@decipher.com
(rules questions, etc.)

DCustServe@decipher.com
(customer service questions)

Computer Networks

Many commercial computer networks
such as CompuServe or America Online
have discussion folders and chat rooms
where you can discuss all aspects of the
game, as well as similar games. Each net-
work has at least one netrep who
represents Decipher, Inc., and who can
answer your questions. Check with your
system operators to learn the name of
your local netrep.

Other Sources of Information

For those without the convenient computer access to such information, there are
many other ways to get the news.

Retailers

One good source is your local retailer,
where you purchased the game or who

carries the game. Most retailers try to keep up to date on the latest information, or can at least point you in the right direction. Decipher will communicate important information to retailers via their quarterly newsletter, "Cosmic Relief."

Fax-Back

Decipher has set up an experimental "fax-back" system. If you have access to a fax machine, you can have Decipher's fax machine automatically fax to you documents that interest you. Call 1-804-N2D-NEWS, and follow the instructions to have it fax you the index sheet. Then you can call again to have it fax back particular documents.

Snail Mail

Of course, you can always send letters to:

Decipher, Inc.

P.O.Box 56

Norfolk VA 23501-0056 USA

SCRYE

GUIDE TO COLLECTIBLE CARD GAMES

Complete Star Trek: The Next Generation Customizable Card Game® and Magic: The Gathering™ Single Card Prices

The Definitive Price Guide

SOLD IN STORES AROUND THE WORLD

SCRYE, INC. 30617 US HWY 19 N., STE. 700, PALM HARBOR, FL 34684 (813) 785-2113
Magic: The Gathering is a trademark of Wizards of the Coast, Inc. Wizards of the Coast is a registered trademark. Star Trek: The Next Generation is a registered trademark of Paramount Pictures. Star:Trek The Next Generation Customizable Card Game is a trademark of Decipher, Inc.

ALTERNATE

UNIVERSE ™

The door opens in August....

WHERE'S GUINAN?